Small Wonders

TINY TREASURES IN PATCHWORK & APPLIQUÉ

Elizabeth Hamby Carlson

Bothell, Washington

That Patchwork Place is an imprint of
Martingale & Company.

MISSION STATEMENT

We are dedicated to providing quality products and service by working together to inspire creativity and to enrich the lives we touch.

Credits

President . . . . Nancy J. Martin
CEO/Publisher . . . . Daniel J. Martin
Associate Publisher . . . . Jane Hamada
Editorial Director . . . . Mary V. Green
Design and Production Manager . . . Cheryl Stevenson
Technical Editor . . . . Darra Williamson
Copy Editor . . . . Tina Cook
Illustrator . . . . Laurel Strand
Photographer . . . . Brent Kane
Cover and Text Design . . . . Rohani Design

Small Wonders: Tiny Treasures in Patchwork and Appliqué
© 1999 by Elizabeth Hamby Carlson

Martingale & Company
PO Box 118
Bothell, WA 98041-0118 USA
Printed in Canada
03 02 01 00 99 98   6 5 4 3 2 1

Dedication

To my father, Russell S. Hamby, who gave me the confidence to go ahead and try, whether I wanted to be a ski instructor or to write a quilt book; and to my mother, Mary Jo Hamby, who taught me to sew, was kind enough to think even my first quilts were wonderful, and from the time I was twelve, always told me I should write a book. Thank you both for all of that, and for so much more.

Acknowledgments

With many thanks to:

All the gifted teachers, particularly Betty Fairies, Tina Gravatt, and Darra Duffy Williamson, who have so generously shared their expertise with me, and with hundreds of other students.

My many students, from whom I continue to learn, and all the shop owners and quilt guilds who have provided a warm and friendly atmosphere for teaching and learning.

Anna Holland, whose irresistibly charming miniature Baltimore Album quilt, "Mini Madness II," introduced me to the pleasures of freezer paper and gluestick appliqué.

The staff at Martingale & Company, particularly Kathryn Ezell, and Darra Williamson for all their help, patience, and professionalism.

Jean Jarrard, a wonderful friend, who can be counted on to work out thorny "quilt math" problems, and for an encouraging word whenever I really need one.

Dolores Pilla, a talented friend whose beautiful quilts are an inspiration, who is always willing to share her considerable expertise and to help search for "just the right fabric," no matter how far we have to travel.

Lorraine Carter, a good friend and skilled appliqué lady, whose encouragement and willingness to help me make the deadline meant a lot.

Elizabeth Stein, my jolly good friend, who loves England and old teapots as much as I, and who is always there with support, good humor, and many helpful suggestions.

And finally, my daughter Kate and my son Russell, who have encouraged my quilting with patience and a good-natured willingness to have quilts instead of a clean house or dinner, and especially my husband, Ken, who is always there for me. Thank you all so much.

Library of Congress Cataloging-in-Publication Data

Carlson, Elizabeth Hamby,
    Small wonders : tiny treasures in patchwork and appliqué / Elizabeth Hamby Carlson.
        p. cm.
    ISBN 1-56477-250-0
    1. Patchwork—Patterns. 2. Quilting—Patterns.
3. Appliqué—Patterns. 4. Miniature quilts. I. Title.
TT835.C17   1999
746.46'041—dc21   98-43430
                                                  CIP

Contents

Russell's Quilt

by Elizabeth Hamby Carlson, 1978, Littleton, Colorado, 36" × 48"; collection of Russell J. Carlson. My first effort, a well-loved baby quilt, combines appliquéd and embroidered Sunbonnet Sue and Overall Sam blocks with a simple Square Within a Square.

Preface

When I began my first quilt one wintry day in 1978, I had no idea that quiltmaking would become such a big part of my life. Twenty years and many, many quilts later, it has become a passion never far from my thoughts. I can hardly imagine what it would be like to no longer pass the time spent in the dentist's chair, or at a boring meeting, by planning a quilt in my head, right down to the tiniest detail. Of course, I don't actually make every one of the quilts I plan in my head (although I usually buy the fabric for them), but I do make a lot of them. And by the time one is finished, I've usually added several more to the list of "quilts in waiting."

But on that February morning in 1978, all I was thinking about was making a quilt for the baby we expected in six weeks' time. The baby was our second child, Russell, and I remember my excitement as I began his quilt, confident that I could finish it in just six weeks. I'd been inspired by an old Sunbonnet Sue quilt pictured in a library book. I had no instructions to follow, and though I had only a sketchy idea of how to proceed, my lack of technical expertise did not deter me. I knew how to sew, and I knew I would figure out how to make it all come together.

My first step was to pay a visit to a local quilt shop. As soon as I laid eyes on all that wonderful fabric I should have realized I was hooked. Totally overwhelmed, I bought enough fabric, not only for the quilt, but for crib bumpers, pillows, and a small table cover as well. No doubt about it, a fabrica-holic was born that morning.

Now when I speak to quilt guilds, I often begin with Russell's baby quilt, because it was my first quilt and because many common threads tie it to the quilts I'm still making all these years later. The antique quilts that drew me to quiltmaking then still inspire me today, and the basic plan I chose for Russell's crib quilt is not unlike many of the quilts I make now. The pattern is traditional and includes both piecing and appliqué. The scale is on the small side: the blocks are only 5" square. Without a teacher to show me the "right" way, I devised my own amateurish versions of the techniques I still prefer: machine piecing, hand appliqué, and hand quilting. I liked doing the appliqué blocks best, and appliqué remains my favorite part of quiltmaking. While the workmanship in Russell's quilt may not bear close inspection, I tried hard, and I finished it on time, fashioning it with the love and care I still try to put into all my quilts. Truly, "the more things change, the more they stay the same."

Introduction

Small things hold a special fascination for me, so I enjoy the challenge of piecing and appliquéing little blocks. I have made many large quilts to cover my family's beds and snuggle up in, but even as I work on a large-scale quilt, I'm thinking about how much fun it would be to make the same quilt again, on a much smaller scale. Sometimes I do make a smaller version of a larger quilt, but more often I skip the large quilt and get right to the small one!

Small quilts require a smaller investment in time and fabric than full-size quilts. Even when intricately appliquéd and quilted, a smaller quilt takes less time to complete, so my enthusiasm for the project is less likely to wear out before the quilt is finished. Like the closets of many other quilters, mine holds several large quilt tops that I tired of before I quilted them. This seldom happens with a small quilt that can be quilted in a short time. I am still eager to see it come alive as I quilt it, and a finished quilt is much more satisfying than yet another unfinished object (UFO) in the closet! Working on a small scale helps me turn more of the quilts in my head into real quilts for my family and friends to enjoy.

Small quilts are easy to manage and they fit nicely on my cutting table. Small, machine-pieced blocks go together quickly, allowing more time for the hand appliqué and hand quilting that are my favorite parts of the process.

When I first learned to appliqué I had difficulty managing tiny pieces, so I compromised by embroidering them instead. Then, in 1986, I purchased Virginia quilter Anna Holland's pattern for a miniature Baltimore Album quilt with blocks measuring only 4½". Anna's directions for appliquéing with freezer-paper templates and a gluestick allowed me to successfully appliqué pieces smaller than I ever thought possible. Since then, I have appliquéd thousands of tiny pieces and have shared with hundreds of students my own tips for achieving accuracy, smooth curves, and sharp points.

Whether tucked in a child's chair with a well loved doll, displayed on a table with a treasured old teapot, or hung on the wall, these small quilts add a warm, personal touch to a home. Designing and making them has filled many happy hours. It is my pleasure to share my methods and my quilts with you. I enjoyed making them all and I hope you will too.

How to Use This Book

Before you begin making the quilts, I encourage you to read the general directions found in the front of this book. In addition to appliqué and piecing techniques, you will find tips on fabric selection, quilt design, and finishing methods that will help you create a small quilt to make you proud.

When making a quilt, please read through all the step-by-step directions before cutting. The measurements have been checked for accuracy, but *always measure your work before cutting borders and squaring up appliqué blocks*. For quick reference when cutting and sewing, use a felt-tip pen to highlight important numbers and measurements. That old rule about not writing in books shouldn't apply to quilt books. Highlight or underline whatever helps you follow the pattern more easily.

Making small quilts is fun, especially when you take your time, enjoy the process, and remember that, in the end, the only person you need to please is yourself!

Choosing Fabric

Think of fabric selection as an opportunity to make your quilt unique. When I choose fabric for a quilt, my creative challenge is: "Which fabrics will make the finished quilt look like the quilt I see in my head?" The quilt in my head will certainly look different from the quilt in your head, but understanding the process I go through to achieve my goal may help you create the quilt you imagine.

COLOR AND MOOD

Color is a quilt's most powerful element, the element that first gets our attention and draws us in. Response to color is a very personal thing. Many quilters find they have a strong preference for particular color plans, for colors they think of as "their" colors. They use these colors over and over again, exploring many variations on the same theme.

I have tried a few times over the years to make quilts in colors that I don't think of as "my" colors. They never seem to work out very well, and often end up as UFOs. Try as I might, I just don't feel enthusiastic about them. Using colors you love to look at and work with will make your quilting time pleasurable, and best of all, you'll have a quilt you are happy to live with. There are always new ways to look at a familiar, favorite color plan.

One way to get started is to choose a multicolored fabric with colors that appeal to you, and use it as a palette fabric. Fabrics that go well with the palette fabric will generally work well together in your quilt, whether or not you use the palette fabric itself. To add depth and interest to your quilt, select fabrics both lighter (tints) and darker (shades) than the colors in the palette fabric. "Teapot Traditions" (page 40) was built around a palette fabric, which forms the outer border.

Sometimes the quilt pattern itself suggests—or at least narrows down—possible color choices. "Christmas Cookies" (page 34) seemed to call for traditional reds and greens, while the soft pastels of an English garden felt right for "Grandmother's Trellis Garden" (page 36).

Besides considering the quilt's color plan, I consider the look or mood I want the quilt to have. I then choose fabrics that help create that mood, and reject those that might disrupt it. For a quilt with an antique or period feel, I look to the many reproduction fabrics available. Bridal Wreath, for example, was a popular pattern in the 1930s, so I used reproduction fabrics to give my new quilt a thirties look (page 40).

Sometimes a fabric may be just the right color but the wrong mood. A contemporary geometric print would not fit the primitive, country look of "Animal Crackers" (page 33), just as a homespun plaid would look out of place in the romantic "Teapot Traditions" (page 40).

VALUE AND SCALE

Value refers to the lightness or darkness of a color. It is hard to overstate the importance of value when making a small quilt with tiny pieces. The placement of value affects the look of a quilt as much or more than color, so it should be considered carefully. The contrast between small pieces needs to be strong. If you place two small pieces of different colors but similar value next to each other, they can easily blend together. If one piece is much darker than the other, however, each piece will be clearly defined. When you take the time to piece or appliqué lots of little pieces, you certainly want your efforts to show! Many of the quilts in this book have very light background fabrics, so the light to medium values used for the appliquéd and pieced patterns show up well, but the quilts still have a soft look. Using very dark background fabrics and very bright lights for the appliquéd and pieced patterns, or light backgrounds with very dark or bright appliqués, would create a more dramatic look.

In addition to the value contrast between different fabrics, look at the value contrast within each fabric itself. A high-contrast fabric, such as one with clearly defined white flowers on a dark background, can be distracting, drawing more attention than you'd like.

Varying the scale and style of prints adds visual texture and makes your quilt more interesting. You may be surprised at how many different types of fabrics you can use, even in a quilt with very small pieces. The key is to be thoughtful, and a little clever, in where and how you use them.

Tone-on-tone prints contain varying shades of one color. They work particularly well in small quilts. Though they often "read" as solids, tone-on-tone prints provide subtle texture. In addition, these forgiving fabrics disguise little mistakes in piecing and appliqué that tend to show up more on solid fabric. Tone-on-tone prints come in a great variety of scales. For small-scale piecing, especially strip piecing, look for small, fairly dense designs. Avoid obviously one-way, linear, or geometric patterns. Little squiggles or foliage patterns are good. For appliqué especially, the pattern in the fabric often can be used to good effect. The leaf print in a green tone-on-tone, for example, might be used for a realistic leaf appliqué.

When shopping for fabric, it is easy to be drawn to pretty little multicolored floral prints. These may seem just right for small quilts, but they must be placed carefully. When cut in small pieces and placed next to each other, the colors in these prints often blur muddily together, and the pattern of the print itself can be distracting. These prints are most effective when used in a piece large enough to showcase a good bit of the pattern, such as in a border, or in small to medium-size pieces surrounded by tone-on-tones.

Medium-scale prints work well as palette fabrics and can be especially good for borders. Large-scale prints may seem unsuitable at first, but try looking at them in a different light. A small section of a large-scale print might be just right for a shaded appliqué piece.

Other fabric categories include plaids, stripes, geometrics, and picture prints. Used with care, these fabrics can add texture and mood to your quilt. They are most easily used for pieces that are cut individually, rather than randomly rotary cut.

To see how a tiny piece of fabric will look in your quilt, try viewing it "through the window." Make a window template by cutting a hole the size and shape of the finished piece in the middle of an index card. When you view the fabric through the template, you will be better able to evaluate how a small piece of that fabric will look in your quilt.

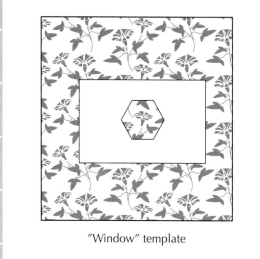

"Window" template

DESIGN WALL

More than anything else, a design wall enables me to create the "quilt in my head." It allows me to stand back and view my work at a distance and try out many different fabric possibilities.

For a small quilt, a design wall can be as simple as a 1½-yard piece of neutral-colored flannel or lightweight batting taped to a wall or stretched over a large piece of cardboard. Fabric will adhere to the surface, just like the flannel board with felt letters and numbers you may remember from your kindergarten days.

With a design wall you can experiment and design your quilt as you go. You can arrange and rearrange blocks and borders, auditioning different fabrics. I often make a mock-up block on my wall, cutting the pieces actual size (without seam allowances), to get a true idea of how the finished block will look. If I'm not happy with something I see, I keep auditioning and rearranging fabric until I am. Better to use a bit of fabric in a mock-up than to waste time and fabric sewing blocks that disappoint you. Remember: just because you cut it doesn't mean you have to sew it! Once the blocks or sections of the quilt are sewn, you can use the wall to position them and to test border fabrics, viewing the quilt upright and at a distance until you are satisfied.

FABRIC PREPARATION

Use 100% cotton fabric for quiltmaking. I pre-wash all the fabric before beginning a project, and I test it for bleeding as well. Most of the fabric sold in quilt shops is of high quality, so bleeding is an infrequent problem, but I'd rather be safe than sorry. My appliqué method often requires soaking the finished blocks to remove glue and freezer paper, so I want to be sure the colors won't run.

There are many ideas on the proper way to prewash and test fabric. I begin by washing like colors together in the washing machine. I use cold water (just as I would to wash the finished quilt) and a small amount of my usual bleach-free family laundry detergent. Clipping the corners off the selvages helps keep the fabric from raveling in the machine.

Next, I place the fabric in the dryer on a medium setting. I remove it before it is completely dry to make it easier to press. Before pressing, I clip a small swatch to test for bleeding. Usually I test several fabrics at a time, soaking the swatches in a glass of cold water, then lining them up on a piece of muslin (or the background fabric I plan to use in the quilt) until completely dry. When the swatches are dry, I check to see if any of them left color on the muslin. Usually, there is no problem, but if there is, I repeat the washing process and test again. If a fabric continues to bleed, I substitute another fabric. I press the fabric before storing it on my shelves, and again before I use it. Precision is especially important when sewing small pieces, and it is impossible to cut wrinkled fabric with precision.

Appliquéing Small Quilts

Appliqué is my first love in quilting. When I need instant gratification or a quilt to actually cover a bed, I will hurriedly construct a machine-pieced quilt. At heart, however, I am an appliquér more than a piecer. Flowing, curving shapes appeal to me more than straight lines and angles, so my quilt designs usually begin with an idea for appliqué, then I add piecework to frame the appliqué blocks.

Appliqué can be more free and easy than piecing. It requires some precision, but not as much as piecing, and that suits my often imprecise mind. I can be careful and precise when absolutely necessary, but I wouldn't want to have to be that way all the time. It's nice to know that if a leaf tilts a little more to the right than I'd planned, it won't throw off the measurement of the whole block.

It's fun to appliqué small blocks, and you'll be surprised at how little time they take. After all, you don't have to sew very far! Before you know it, a block is done and you're on to the next one. If tiny pieces seem daunting, I encourage you to try the appliqué methods in this book, which have worked well for me and for my students. Your success may surprise you!

HAND APPLIQUÉ

The peaceful repetition of hand appliqué is soothing. I find I have a different mind-set when doing handwork. At the machine, I'm always in a hurry to be done, but when sewing by hand, I relax and enjoy the process, taking pleasure in the look and feel of the fabric as I stitch.

Tools and Supplies

Have you ever had a repairman come to your home, and then realized you could have easily done the job yourself, had you only known about—or had access to—the special tool he used? The correct tool can be an important trick of the trade, whether you are making a home repair or making a quilt. It can be difficult to cut tiny appliqué shapes accurately with 8", none-too-sharp sewing shears, or to appliqué tiny pieces with needles meant for mending sturdy clothing. The wrong tool will only frustrate you. Treat yourself to the right tools, and keep them in good condition. Your sewing time will be more pleasant and successful.

Scissors: For cutting fabric appliqués you'll need *sharp* scissors that cut cleanly, right to the tip. My favorites are approximately 5" long, a good size for most appliqué projects. Reserve your appliqué scissors for fabric only. Use another pair of small scissors for cutting freezer paper and plastic templates.

Rotary-cutting equipment: A rotary cutter, cutting mat, and gridded acrylic ruler are useful for cutting and squaring up appliqué blocks.

Freezer paper: Ordinary freezer paper, found at the grocery store, is ideal for appliqué templates and is also handy for making long border patterns. When pressed onto fabric, the plastic coating causes the paper to adhere, but it is easily removed and leaves no residue.

Plastic template material: When I need to cut many freezer-paper templates of the same shape, I first make a plastic template of the shape. The hard plastic edge makes tracing fast and accurate, and the freezer-paper templates are more uniform than those traced from paper. Look for flexible template plastic. The more flexible it is, the easier it will be to cut in smooth curves. If you are able to get it, X-ray film is ideal.

Gluestick: Your gluestick should be water soluble so that when the appliqué block is soaked, the glue will rinse out. You can try several different brands of gluestick and choose the one you like best. The glue in some brands has a glassy, frosty look, while in others the glue is milky white and pasty. I like the glassy, frosty type best, finding it easier to apply to the fabric, while the milky white types seem gummier. This is a matter of personal preference, so if you aren't having good results with one brand, try another and use what works best. Just be sure the glue rinses out of the fabric easily in cold water. It's a good idea to test a new brand before using it on your quilt.

Fine-line permanent pen: These pens are useful for tracing freezer-paper templates, for drawing a fine turn-under line on appliqué fabric, and for drawing and writing on quilts. Make sure the pen really is permanent before you use it on your quilt.

Water-soluble marking pen: I use these erasable felt-tip pens to mark the appliqué pattern on the background block when I use freezer-paper appliqué with glue. When I soak the finished block to remove the glue and freezer paper, the marks disappear. To be certain that all residue is removed, use these markers only when the block is to be fully immersed in water. *Never iron a block until the marks have been completely removed.* As with any marking tool, test it on your fabric before using it.

Light table: Use a light table, or light box, when tracing the appliqué pattern onto background fabric or when placing appliqué pieces on an unmarked block. It's easy to make a light table by removing the leaf from an extension table, placing a piece of glass or Plexiglas over the opening, and putting a lamp on the floor under the table. Lightweight light tables, designed for quilters, are available in many quilt shops.

Thread: Thread should match the color of the appliqué piece as closely as possible. If you can't find an exact match, use thread that is a shade darker rather than lighter. Use 100% cotton thread, or cotton-covered polyester. You may wish to experiment with different threads. Some 100% cotton threads are hard to thread onto very fine needles; cotton-covered polyester tends to thread more easily. If you are using all-cotton thread, look for an appliqué needle with a larger eye, or try a needle threader. Run the thread over thread wax to strengthen it and help keep it from tangling.

Needles: For appliqué, you'll need a long, fine needle. I prefer needles that are fairly flexible as well. The size 11 Sharp is a good all-purpose appliqué needle. I sometimes use a longer, size 10 Sharp for needle-turn appliqué. Some brands are easier to thread than others, so you may wish to experiment.

Pins: Pins should be very fine. I use extra-fine silk pins. Some quilters like to use sequin pins for appliqué—because they are very short, the thread is less likely to catch on them. To avoid catching thread on the pins, you can pin appliqué pieces to the background from the wrong side of the block.

Orange stick: This thin wooden stick with a beveled tip (like a screwdriver's tip), is normally used by manicurists but is very handy for gluestick appliqué as well. I use one to hold little pieces in place while applying glue, to pick up glue-covered pieces, and to turn the edges of appliqué pieces over the edges of freezer-paper templates.

Tracing paper: Use tracing paper to make appliqué placement overlays (see "Preparing Background Fabric" on page 13) and for tracing asymmetrical freezer-paper templates (see "Making Freezer-Paper Templates" on pages 14–15).

Lap pillow: Using a lap pillow for hand sewing is a trick I learned from one of my students. The pillow elevates the work a bit and provides a place to rest my hands and smooth my block. I can pin little pieces on it to keep track of them, and when I'd like my work to be portable, I put all the little pieces in a zipper-lock bag and pin the bag to the pillow! My pillow measured 12" × 18" before stuffing, and it is stuffed very hard. The plain muslin top doesn't distract from whatever work I have on it. The lady who made my pillow embroidered it with the words "my third hand," and it really is just that.

Preparing Background Fabric

Background blocks for appliqué should be cut carefully so that the sides of the block are parallel to the lengthwise grain. When the blocks are set together in the quilt, the lengthwise grain should run consistently from top to bottom so the finished quilt will hang flat and square. Lightly mark a tiny grain-line arrow in the seam allowance of each block to remind you which side of the block is the top.

As you work on the block, it may fray and pieces may shift, so cut it at least 1" larger than the desired finished size. When the block is finished, trim and square it to the finished measurement plus ½" to allow for ¼" seam allowances on all sides. (See "Squaring Up the Blocks" on page 25.)

One way to place appliqué pieces on the background block is to mark the appliqué design directly on the block. If you are willing to soak the completed appliqué block in water, you can use a water-soluble pen to mark the design. These pens are easy to mark with and easy to see. When the block is soaked in cold, clear water, the marks disappear. It's necessary to soak the block to completely remove the marks. If you prefer not to soak the block, use as few markings as possible. Pencils may not wash out easily, and it is difficult to make appliqué shapes fit the pattern so precisely

that they completely cover the marks. Use a pencil you have tested to be sure you can remove the marks. Mark lightly and as little as possible. For example, mark a single line for placement of a vine, and just a dot to indicate where the point of a leaf goes.

If your fabric is very light, simply lay it over the pattern and trace the design. If you cannot see the pattern through the fabric, place the pattern on a light table, center your background block over it, and trace.

To place appliqué pieces without marking the background, you'll need to make an overlay. This is a good method to use with needleturn appliqué, in which you turn under the edges of the appliqué with the needle as you stitch. To make an overlay, cut a piece of tracing paper or clear vinyl 1" larger than the appliqué block and trace the design onto it. Cut a piece of sturdy cardboard 2" larger than the appliqué block. Use tape or staples to hinge the upper edge of the paper or vinyl to the upper edge of the cardboard. To position appliqué pieces, lay the background block on the cardboard, underneath the traced design, then position the appliqués so they align with the tracing.

Freezer Paper and Gluestick Appliqué

For basting, I like to use glue instead of thread. One advantage of this method is that the appliqués are their finished size and shape before they are sewn to the block. You can prepare all the pieces for a block and preview them before stitching. If you aren't happy with something, it's easy to change it. Remember: just because you cut it doesn't mean you have to sew it.

Making Freezer-Paper Templates

Because the appliqué pieces in these quilts are very small, accurate paper templates are essential. The shape you cut is the shape you get!

Trace each appliqué piece onto the dull side of freezer paper. If the block has pieces of many different sizes, mark the piece number on each template. Use a fine-line permanent pen for tracing, so that any marks left on the paper template will not run when you soak the completed block to remove the glue. Cut out the paper templates right on the marked line.

Note: *When the appliqué pattern is asymmetrical, the templates must be reversed or the design will appear as a mirror image of the design on the quilt. For example, if the teapots in "Teapot Traditions" weren't reversed, they would face opposite those shown in the photo on page 40. To reverse templates, copy them onto a piece of tracing paper, then trace them from the wrong side of the tracing paper (method 1). Or use a light box to trace templates from the back (method 2).*

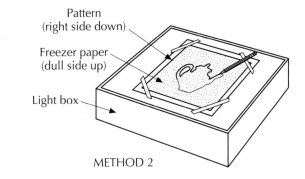

METHOD 2

To increase speed and accuracy when cutting many templates for the same shape, make a plastic window template. Use the window template to trace the shape repeatedly onto freezer paper. For tracing circles, a circle template, available in art-supply stores, is very handy.

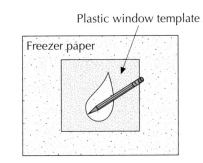

Plastic window template
Freezer paper

To trace and cut a symmetrical shape, such as a heart, align half the shape with the fold on a piece of folded freezer paper. Trace and cut on the fold, just as you did when making valentines in elementary school. If you need to cut many paper templates of the same symmetrical shape, make a plastic template of half the shape. For very small pieces, leave a tab of plastic to hold while tracing the half-shape.

Tracing Reverse Appliqué Patterns

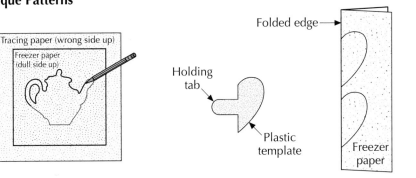

Pattern (right side up)
Tracing paper

Tracing paper (wrong side up)
Freezer paper (dull side up)

METHOD 1

Folded edge
Holding tab
Plastic template
Freezer paper

For patterns requiring many of the same template, you can trace half the number needed by doubling the layers of freezer paper before you cut. Staple the layers together to prevent shifting. To maintain accuracy, however, don't double the paper when cutting on a fold—trace each piece individually.

Cutting the Appliqués

Place the freezer-paper templates on the wrong side of the appliqué fabric with the dull side of the paper up. Leave room for a ³⁄₁₆" seam allowance around each piece. Place shapes with points, like leaves, so that the points are on the bias. This will make turning the seam allowance easier. If there is a motif in the fabric you wish to feature, feel free to ignore the grain line.

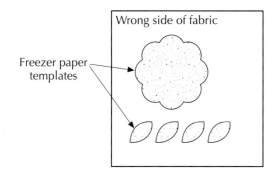

Press with a hot, dry iron; the shiny side of the freezer paper will adhere to the fabric.

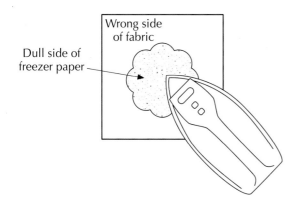

After you've cut out a freezer-paper template, use the "leavings" of the paper as a window template. When placed on fabric, the window will show you just how the finished piece would look.

The standard seam allowance for appliqué is ³⁄₁₆". A ¼" seam allowance is too much, especially for small pieces, and less than ⅛" is not enough, even for the smallest pieces. I cut seam allowances between ³⁄₁₆" and ⅛", reserving the narrower allowance for tiny pieces and needleturn appliqué. If you are new to appliqué, use ³⁄₁₆" on all your pieces until you get a feel for what works best. Add the seam allowance around each piece as you cut.

When one edge of an appliqué piece will be layered under another, allow a tiny bit of extra seam allowance on that edge to make placement easier. Any excess can be trimmed later. Do not clip into the seam allowances.

Glue Basting the Appliqués

To catch excess glue, place the appliqué pieces on a flat surface covered with scrap paper. I usually work on a lap board and use the pages of old mail-order catalogs as scrap paper. When one page is covered with glue, I just turn the page.

Spread the glue over the seam allowance of each piece. On small pieces, the glue may cover the whole piece. Do not glue an edge that will lie under another piece, as that edge will not need to be basted. It is easier to turn the seam allowances after the glue has dried for several minutes; this allows you to glue many pieces at once.

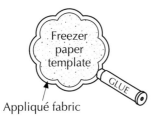

Freezer paper template
Appliqué fabric
GLUE

After applying the glue, clip seam allowances on inside curves and inside points to within one thread of the paper. Do not clip outside curves or outside points.

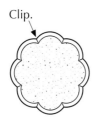

Clip.

You can use either your fingers or a wooden orange stick to turn the seam allowance. I use my fingers for simple shapes and a stick for complex ones like the teapots in "Teapot Traditions" (page 40). If using your fingers, hold the piece up so the right side faces you; if using a stick, leave the piece flat, wrong side up.

If there is an inside point or curve, begin there by folding the fabric over the edge of the paper. Fold only a small bit of fabric at a time. On outside curves, make tiny pleats as you fold the fabric over the paper, as you would when crimping a piecrust.

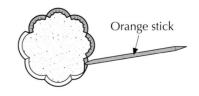

Orange stick

Once you have achieved a smooth edge, flatten the seam allowance into little pleats on the back. If you turned the edges over with your fingers, lay the piece flat and use an orange stick to smooth out the back of the piece.

Sharp outside points can be handled in two ways. The traditional way is to miter the point. First, fold the point of the fabric toward the appliqué. Next, fold the right side, then the left side toward the center of the appliqué to form a point.

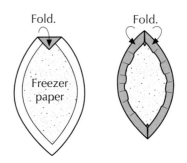

Fold.   Fold.
Freezer paper

On a very small piece with two outside points, mitering the points can make it difficult to turn a smooth curve between them. For extra-small leaves, try this instead: fold one edge of the fabric leaf over the template, extending the fold beyond the points of the paper on each end.

Fold the other side in the same way. The leaf will have smooth curves and sharp points, with a little "flag" of fabric sticking out at each point.

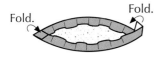

Fold the flags behind each point and press with your fingers or an orange stick. There will probably be enough glue to hold the flags in place. If not, leave them sticking out for now. You can push them behind the point with your needle when you appliqué the piece to the background.

Fold.   Fold.

Stitching the Appliqués

Appliqué the pieces to the background with the traditional appliqué stitch. Use a single strand of thread that closely matches the appliqué. To hide the starting knot, slip the needle between the paper template and the seam allowance on the wrong side of the appliqué, then bring the needle through the folded edge of the appliqué.

Make the first stitch by inserting the needle into the background fabric, just under the edge of the appliqué and below the spot where the needle emerged. The thread does not travel forward or backward on the front of the block but goes straight down off the appliqué.

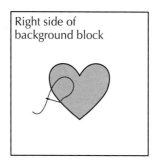

Run the needle not more than ⅛" under the background fabric, parallel to the edge of the appliqué. Bring the needle up through the background fabric, catching one or two threads on the folded edge of the appliqué.

On the front, all you see is a tiny dot of thread where each stitch is taken, while on the back, the thread runs almost parallel to the appliqué edge. To end off, take two stitches behind the appliqué, close to the stitching line, and bring the needle through the loop.

Although the paper is still inside the piece, for the most part you will not stitch through it. The needle will just nick the edge of the paper as you stitch. (When the papers are removed, the edges will look as though they were perforated.) If you do sew through the paper, as you might at an inside point, don't worry. The paper will come out easily when the block is soaked.

Inside and outside points need special attention. As you near an inside point, make your tiny stitches even shorter. At the point of the **V**, take a deeper bite into the appliqué fabric, bringing the needle out three or four threads inside the folded edge. Take two or three stitches at the **V**, right next to each other, almost like a satin stitch. As you stitch away from the point, continue to keep your stitches very small.

When stitching toward an outside point, make very small stitches to secure the point and to keep any stray threads or frayed edges out of sight. If a flag of fabric is visible, stitch up one side, right to the point, tuck the flag behind the point with the needle, then sew down the other side with tiny stitches.

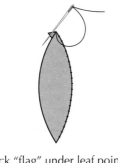

Tuck "flag" under leaf point
with needle.

To layer one piece on top of another, sew the top piece to the bottom piece, stitching only through the bottom piece. Do not stitch through the paper in the bottom piece.

Removing the Glue and Freezer Paper

When the appliqué is complete, carefully snip a portion of the background fabric behind each appliqué to expose the paper template. Do not cut within ⅛" of the stitching line.

Wrong side of
background block

Soak the block in cold, clear water for at least ten minutes to rinse out the glue and soften the paper. Any water-erasable pen lines will disappear quickly. Take the block from the water and carefully remove the paper from each piece with tweezers. Where pieces are layered, remove the paper from the bottom piece first, then cut into the bottom piece to remove the paper from the top piece.

Wrong side of
background block

Rinse the block thoroughly in cold water. Roll it in a thick white towel and blot, removing as much moisture as possible to prevent possible bleeding. Lay the block flat to dry. I lay wet blocks over a wooden drying rack so that air circulates freely, allowing the blocks to dry faster. When the block is completely dry, steam press it from the wrong side, placing a thick white towel under the block to avoid crushing the appliqué.

OTHER FREEZER-PAPER METHODS

At times, you may not want to use glue to prepare appliqué pieces. You may find the glue inconvenient or unavailable, or you may not wish to soak your work to remove the glue and paper. Happily, there are other ways to use freezer paper for appliqué.

Instead of basting appliqué edges over the paper with glue, you can baste them with needle and thread. This method can be a little tricky with very small or intricately shaped pieces, but it eliminates soaking the block to remove the paper.

Make paper templates and press them to the fabric, just as you would for glue basting. Fold the edges of the fabric over the paper and thread-baste, clipping inside points and curves as needed.

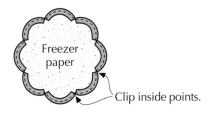

Once the appliqué is sewn to the background, simply remove the basting thread, snip the background fabric behind the piece, and remove the paper with tweezers.

Appliqué pieces prepared with freezer-paper templates can also be needle-turned. The paper template provides a crisp edge for turning and requires no markings on the appliqué piece itself. Pin—or baste, if the piece is large—the appliqué to the background. Appliqué the piece in place, turning under the seam allowance with the side of the needle as you go. To keep curves smooth, turn under only a tiny bit at a time. Remove the paper by cutting into

the background behind the piece or by pulling the paper out just before the piece is completely sewn.

STEMS AND VINES

Here is an easy method for appliquéing narrow stems and vines that doesn't require any special tools.

Rotary cut bias strips a scant ½" wide. I usually don't bother to measure the length precisely; I just cut plenty and trim as needed. Press under approximately ³⁄₁₆" along one long edge.

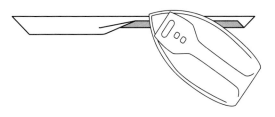

To attach the vine, appliqué the folded edge in place, then stitch the other side, turning under the raw edge with the needle as you go. If the vine is circular, stitch the folded edge on the *inside* of the circle first. For sharp curves, sew the concave (or inner) edge of the curve first whenever possible.

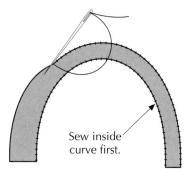

Sew inside curve first.

Piecing with Precision

Ten years ago, a friend and I had a little business selling machine-pieced miniature, and not quite miniature, quilts. Because we hoped to make a profit (and have a great excuse to buy lots of fabric), we had a strong incentive to develop timesaving methods while maintaining quality. The business itself was short-lived, as we quickly tired of producing the same quilts over and over again. But the timesaving techniques and tips we learned have proven useful to me and to my students.

The pieced portions of the quilts in this book are made up of small—sometimes very small—pieces. Small-scale quilts require even more precision than similar large-scale quilts. The pieced Schoolhouse block in "School Days" (page 37) for example, has eight seams across its width. If each seam is off by just $\frac{1}{16}$", the block will be a full $\frac{1}{2}$" too wide. This is too much to ease in when setting a quilt with $3\frac{1}{2}$" blocks! So, when I piece, I try to ensure precision at each step.

TOOLS AND SUPPLIES

Just as with appliqué, it's important to use the right tool for the job.

Rotary cutter and mat: To accurately cut small pieces and narrow strips, you need a good quality rotary cutter with a sharp blade. There are several brands available, so experiment until you find one that is comfortable for you. A rotary mat with grid lines helps you keep fabric square when cutting. But never use the grid lines for measuring. Always measure with your ruler.

Rotary rulers: A ruler with continuous $\frac{1}{8}$" markings is handy for working with small pieces. I like the 3" × 18" Omnigrid ruler. I also use the Bias Square® ruler for making half-square triangle units and squaring up small blocks.

Sewing machine: Your sewing machine needn't have a lot of fancy features, but it should be in good working order and stitch a straight stitch with even tension.

Quilters' sewing machine foot: Many sewing machine manufacturers make a $\frac{1}{4}$"-wide foot that allows quilters to align the edge of the fabric with the foot and maintain an accurate $\frac{1}{4}$" seam allowance. If a special foot isn't available, try using an old-fashioned straight-stitch foot. Years ago, before sewing machines could zigzag, the standard sewing foot was narrower on both sides of the needle than the all-purpose foot on today's machines. The narrower width to the left of the needle makes it easier to piece narrow strips together and keep them straight.

Seam ripper, small screwdriver, or stiletto: Use one of these tools to guide small pieces under the presser foot. The seam ripper's tip can go where your fingers cannot, and should not! Use it to ease fabric and adjust seam allowances that want to flip the wrong way.

Machine needles: Use a fresh, sharp needle in your machine in a size suited to the thread and fabric.

Thread: For machine piecing I use a neutral-colored 100% cotton sewing thread. Light gray blends well with most fabrics. If your fabrics are very dark, use darker thread.

Spray starch: When working with small pieces, spray starch is my not-so-secret weapon. I starch and press fabric before cutting to give it more body. When strip piecing, I starch the sewn and pressed strip sets before cutting them into units or rows to make the small pieces easier to handle.

ROTARY CUTTING

For the quilts in this book, most of the pieced sections can be cut quickly and accurately with a rotary cutter.

When you need small pieces or short strips and you have a yard or more of fabric, first rough-cut a more manageable piece of fabric. Handling a large, heavy length of fabric when you need only a bit can be awkward and might result in inaccurate cutting. Press the fabric with spray starch before rotary cutting to make it crisper and easier to mark and cut.

Whenever possible, cut strips on the lengthwise grain of the fabric, parallel to the selvage edge. To see why, take a piece of fabric and pull it on the crossgrain, from selvage to selvage. You will see that there is quite a bit of stretch. When you pull the fabric on the lengthwise grain, parallel to the selvage edge, there is little, if any, stretch.

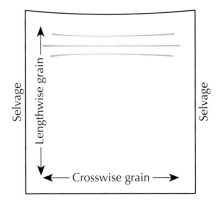

Strips cut lengthwise are the most stable and therefore the easiest to piece accurately. For small-scale piecing, a "fat quarter"—an 18" × 22" piece with the 18" length along the selvage edge—is often more useful than a traditional quarter-yard cut, which has only 9" along the selvage edge.

To maintain accuracy while cutting and sewing, cut strips no longer than 18". You can fold an 18" length of fabric in half so the actual cut is only 9" long. You can even layer two fabrics and cut through four folded layers, but you must have a very sharp blade in your cutter or the layers will

shift. When cutting very narrow strips, it is best to cut no more than two layers at a time.

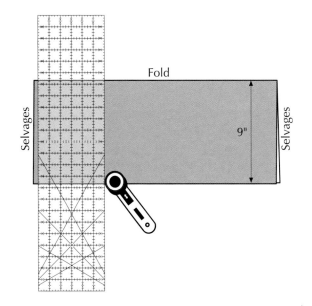

Some of the quilts in this book call for bias strips. Bias strips are cut at a 45-degree angle to the selvage edge of the fabric. When cutting bias strips, use a rotary ruler with a 45-degree angle marked on it. To get a clean, straight fabric edge, use your rotary cutter and ruler to remove the selvage. Align the 45-degree line on the ruler with cut edge, then cut along the ruler's long edge. The cut edge will be a bias edge.

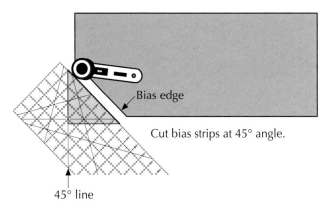

Cut bias strips at 45° angle.

ACCURATE PIECING

When I learned to piece miniature quilts, I was taught to use a ⅛" seam allowance. For some years I continued to use—and taught students to use—

⅛" seam allowances for most small projects. Because there was so little margin for error, I learned to be very precise indeed! Several years of teaching miniature and small-scale piecing convinced me, however, that using ¼" seam allowances was easier and more manageable for most quilters, and for their sewing machines. Therefore, all the pieced patterns in this book are sewn with ¼" seam allowances, which you'll trim after sewing to reduce bulk.

An accurate seam allowance is the key to success in small-scale piecing. Without an accurate seam allowance, your pieces won't finish to the correct size. Inaccurate pieces become inaccurate blocks—a sure recipe for disaster.

To achieve an accurate seam allowance, make a seam guide for your sewing machine.

1. Place either ¼" graph paper or the ¼" mark on a rotary ruler directly under the needle on your machine. Lower the needle until it pierces the first ¼" marking on the paper or just touches the ruler. To make sure the ruler or graph paper is straight, align a horizontal line on the machine with a horizontal line on the ruler or graph paper. (The edge of the throat plate makes a good guide.) Then lower the presser foot to hold it in place.

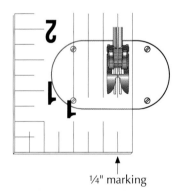

¼" marking

2. Right along the edge of the ruler or paper, just in front of the feed dogs and exactly ¼" to the right of the needle's point, stack several pieces of 1"-long masking tape. Align the long edge that will be your guide. As an alternative, you could use adhesive-backed moleskin, which is sold for foot care. Moleskin is available in two thicknesses. I use

the thinner of the two and cut a ½" × 1" piece. It provides a slightly thick, straight edge and eliminates the need to layer. Cut moleskin seam guides with a rotary cutter (using an old blade) to ensure a clean, straight edge.

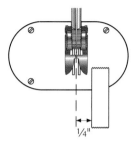

¼"

Make this seam guide even if your machine has a perfect ¼" presser foot. A seam guide that extends in front of the presser foot helps you keep little pieces straight as you feed them through the machine. If you wait until the piece reaches the presser foot to adjust the width of the seam allowance, it may be too late.

To check the accuracy of your seam guide, cut and sew together two 1"-wide strips, one dark and one light. After stitching, measure to be sure the distance from the sewing line to the cut edge is exactly ¼". To be absolutely certain the seam is accurate, make one further test. Press the seam toward the dark strip. Cut an additional 1"-wide dark strip and sew it to the raw edge of the light strip. Press the new seam away from the light strip. If the seam allowances are accurate, the center strip will measure exactly ½" wide. If it doesn't, make certain the seam has been pressed perfectly flat, check your seam guide, and repeat the test until you achieve an accurate ¼" seam allowance.

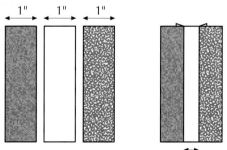

1"   1"   1"

½"

Once you have marked your machine with a seam guide, you are ready to start sewing. Set the stitch length to approximately twelve stitches per inch. Sewing machines differ in the ways they calibrate stitch length, and the setting that gives you twelve stitches per inch may not be obvious. You'll need stitches short enough to hold a short seam together securely but long enough to be picked apart with a seam ripper when necessary.

As you stitch, use a small seam ripper, screwdriver, or stiletto to guide small pieces under the needle and keep them straight. Tiny pieces can be hard to direct, but the seam ripper can keep you firmly in control. Many sewing machines tend to push the pieces a bit to the left as they approach the end of a seam. As a result, the seam allowance "wings out" at the end rather than staying nice and straight all along the seam. You can prevent this by using the seam ripper (in your right hand) and the fingers of your left hand to keep the pieces next to the edge of the seam guide all the way to the end of the seam.

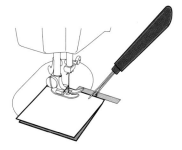

To join two pieces, lay them right sides together. Make sure the raw edges are aligned, then feed the pieces through the machine. There is no need to backstitch because most seams will be crossed by another.

A technique called "chain piecing" can make stitching even more efficient and accurate and can save lots of thread as well. After sewing the first two pieces together, do not break the thread or raise the presser foot. Pick up the next pair of pieces and feed them under the presser foot right after the first ones. They will be connected to the first pair by a chain of thread. Continue chaining

pieces through the machine in this manner, removing the entire chain from the machine when finished. I usually make a chain of all like pairs. Since the chain keeps them together, I can easily keep track of them.

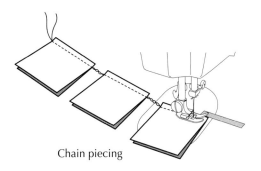

Chain piecing

While chain piecing is a great time-saver, exercise caution. Just as you can sew a large number of pieces correctly in a short time, you can also sew a large number of pieces incorrectly! For that reason, I always check to be sure the first pair is sewn properly. Then I carefully lay out the rest of the pairs to the left of my machine so they will be sewn the same way. It's discouraging to have to "unsew" a long chain of pieces that were sewn speedily on the wrong edge. As a wise quilting teacher once told me, "sometimes slower is faster."

PRESSING TECHNIQUES

Just as it is important to take care when cutting and sewing small pieces, it is important when pressing as well. Improper pressing can distort small blocks, even when they have been perfectly cut and sewn. Do remember that pressing is not the same thing as ironing. Pressing is an up-and-down movement of the iron, while ironing is a back-and-forth movement that can distort small pieces.

Quilters continue to debate whether or not to use steam when pressing. I find that many irons simply do not get hot enough to do the job without steam, so I generally use it. I press carefully and have never had a problem with distortion. If you find otherwise, do whatever works for you. There are no hard-and-fast rules here! With or without steam, use a light touch when pressing small pieces. Small-scale work requires a kind and gentle approach.

Specific pressing directions are included with the instructions for each quilt. Generally, seams are pressed to create opposing seam allowances, with an eye toward the quilting plan. No one wants to hand quilt through unnecessary layers.

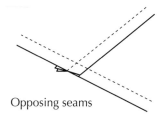

Opposing seams

Seams should first be pressed flat, to set the seam and eliminate any tiny puckers left after sewing. Place the piece you'll press the seam allowance toward on top, with the seam allowance away from you, and press carefully.

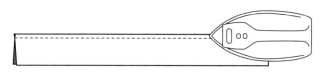

After setting the seam, open the pieces. From the right side, press the seam allowance toward the top piece, taking care to fully open and flatten it. If there is a little tuck in the seam, it will affect the measurement of the finished piece.

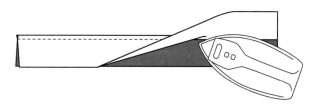

Long strips have a tendency to curve when pressed. Cutting them on the lengthwise grain helps control this, but be sure to keep the strips straight on the ironing surface as you press. *When making strip sets with three or more strips, press each seam before adding another strip to the set.* I give completed strip sets a final press with spray starch before cutting them into units or rows, and I starch bias-strip pairs before marking and cutting squares from them. Bias edges require an especially light touch because they stretch easily. Remember to press, not iron, bias edges!

TRIMMING SEAMS

While sewing with a ¼" seam allowance makes piecing easier, the bulk of all those seams can make a small quilt seem overstuffed, much like an over-sized pot holder! I prefer to trim most seam allowances to approximately ⅛". When you trim, the quilt drapes better and is easier to hand quilt. Trimming the seam allowances also makes it easier to sew narrow strips together.

To trim or not to trim is a matter of judgment. I follow this simple rule: when the block is heavily pieced and/or has tiny pieces or very narrow strips, I trim the seams. When the block is appliquéd or is not heavily pieced, I leave the main seams—those joining the blocks—untrimmed, so I can more easily make any necessary adjustments when setting the quilt. As you follow the patterns in this book, keep these tips in mind.

I trim seams with scissors, after sewing but before pressing. I've tried trimming with a rotary cutter but find it takes more time to lay the pieces out carefully on the cutting table than to trim them with scissors while sitting at the machine. Before trimming a seam, especially a tricky seam with multiple pieces, check to be sure you sewed it correctly. It is harder to correct a sewing mistake after the seams have been trimmed. This is another time to remember "sometimes slower is faster."

Setting the Quilt and Adding Borders

Whenever I set a large quilt together I remember why I prefer making small quilts, and I vow to think twice before embarking on another large project. I enjoy piecing the individual blocks for a large quilt; however, when I must sew the blocks together into ever larger units, I begin to feel that I am not having fun. Maneuvering vast quantities of fabric under the machine has never been my idea of a good time. But a small quilt is another story! All the blocks can be laid on my sewing table and quickly and easily sewn together. There is no wrestling with long runs of fabric and no pressing seams that don't entirely fit on the ironing board. Most small quilts can be set together in an afternoon, often with time to spare.

SQUARING UP THE BLOCKS

Because they are cut larger than necessary, you'll need to square up appliqué blocks before setting them into your quilt. I have seen many students approach this step with trepidation. Rest assured: with a bit of care, it's really quite simple!

Note: Always measure your work. If appliqué blocks alternate with pieced blocks in your quilt, make the pieced blocks before squaring up the appliqué blocks. Measure your pieced blocks, square them up if necessary, then trim the appliqué blocks so they are the same size.

Cut a plastic template the exact size of the block, including seam allowances. Mark the seam lines, center lines, and diagonal lines on the template. Trace the appliqué pattern onto the template. (If the quilt has many blocks of the same size but with different patterns, you needn't make a separate template for each design. The seam, center, and diagonal lines will do.) Center the template over the block, matching the lines as closely as possible. Don't worry if the appliqué pieces have shifted a bit, but be sure they don't run into the seam allowance. Draw a light pencil line around the edges of the template. Cut on the lines with scissors or a rotary cutter.

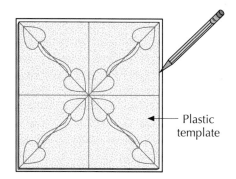

Plastic template

ASSEMBLING THE BLOCKS

Most of the quilts in this book are assembled in a straight set. Lay out the blocks in rows, following the directions and the photo for each quilt. (Even the diagonally set quilts are laid out and sewn in rows. The rows are just diagonal, beginning and ending with triangles.) Sew the blocks together in rows, pressing the seams so they oppose when the rows are joined. For example, if pieced and appliquéd blocks alternate, press all seams toward the appliqué blocks. Sew the rows together, pinning at the beginning and end of each row and at the block intersections.

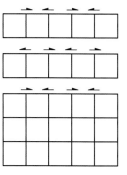

Arrows indicate the direction to press for opposing seams.

For quilts with sashing strips and corner squares, treat the sashing strips and squares as you would a row of blocks.

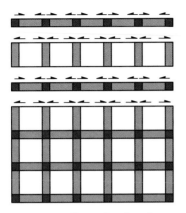

Arrows indicate the direction
to press for opposing seams.

ADDING BORDERS

Two of the quilts in this book have no true borders at all. The others use one of three border plans: straight-cut, plain mitered, or cutwork-appliqué mitered. Border measurements are given in the instructions for each quilt, but as variations may crop up during stitching and pressing, always measure your work before cutting borders.

Straight-Cut Borders

Straight-cut borders are the simplest to make. The side borders are the same length as the body of the quilt and are added first. The top and bottom borders are the width of the quilt body, plus the width of the two side borders. When a quilt has inner and outer straight-cut borders, add the inner border to all four sides of the quilt first, then add the outer borders.

1. Measure the length of the quilt top through its center. Cut side borders of the required width to match this measurement. Use a pin to mark the center of each border strip and the center of each side of the quilt. Pin the borders to the quilt top,

matching the center points and outer edges, then stitch. Press the seam allowances toward the borders.

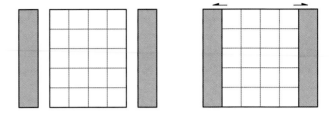

2. Measure the width of the quilt (including the side borders) through its center. Cut top and bottom borders of the required width to match this measurement. Pin and sew the top and bottom borders to the quilt top as described in step 1. Press the seam allowances toward the borders.

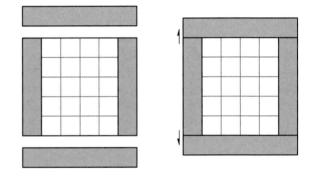

Mitered Borders

Mitered borders require a little more time and attention than straight-cut borders, but they aren't difficult and they give a quilt a polished look. They can be especially effective when striped fabrics are used. Cut miter strips the full length or width of the quilt (including borders), plus an extra inch. When the quilt has more than one border to be mitered, cut all the border strips for each side the same length as the outermost border and sew them together so they can be sewn to the quilt and mitered as a single unit.

There are a number of ways to make mitered borders. Because I like to appliqué, I sew the miters closed by hand. It's a simple method, and because I work from the right side, it's nearly foolproof, especially for multiple or striped borders.

1. Measure the quilt as for straight-cut borders (page 26). Estimate the final outside measurements of the quilt, including the borders, and add 1". Cut the border strips to this length.

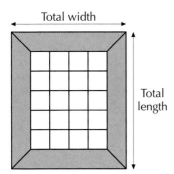

2. Use a pin to mark the center of each border strip and the center of each side of the quilt top. On each border strip, measure and mark one-half the length (or width) of the body of the quilt top from each side of the center pin.

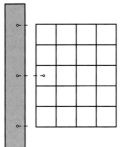

3. Place the border strips and quilt top right sides together, matching the center and outer pins to the raw edges of the quilt top. Sew the border to the quilt top, beginning and ending with a backstitch ¼" from the corners of the quilt top. Press the seams toward the borders. Repeat on each side of the quilt.

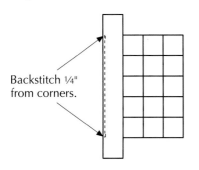

Backstitch ¼" from corners.

4. To make the miters, lay the quilt on an ironing board so the top border extends over the side borders. Fold under one corner of the top border at a 45-degree angle. Use a Bias Square or similar ruler with a 45-degree mark to check that the fold is exactly 45 degrees, all the way to the outer corner. (The angle must be true for the border miters to match the binding miters later.) Press the fold firmly and pin it securely, placing pins perpendicular to the fold.

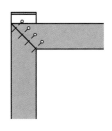

5. Hand sew the miter closed from the right side with tiny, invisible appliqué stitches. This will be a main construction seam in the quilt so sew it carefully. Repeat this process for the remaining three miters, trimming the seams to ¼" and pressing them open.

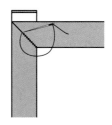

Cutwork Appliqué Borders

Cutwork borders consist of a mitered inner border, usually of background fabric, with an outer, shaped border appliquéd over it. The shaped border extends to the outer edges of the quilt.

1. Make the inner border, following the directions for plain mitered borders on this page.

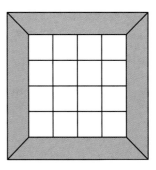

2. If the quilt is square, one border template is used for all sides. If the quilt is rectangular, two border templates are used, one for the sides and another for the top and bottom. Cut a piece of freezer paper twice the length of the border template, plus an inch or two. Fold the freezer paper in half to find the center, and crease. Unfold the paper. Trace the border template onto the freezer paper, matching the fold line on the template to the fold of the paper and aligning the long, straight edge of the paper with the long, straight edge of the border template. Refold the paper and staple the halves together so they won't shift when cut. Cut the paper template.

3. Cut four strips of fabric for the outer shaped border according to the measurements given with the quilt pattern. Fold each strip to find its center and mark it with a pin.

4. Press the paper template onto the right side of an outer border strip, matching center points and aligning the long, straight edge of the template with the outer edge of the border strip. The ends of the fabric should extend an inch or more beyond the ends of the template.

With a sharp pencil, trace the shaped, curved edge of the template onto the fabric. Stop where the miter begins; do not trace the angle of the miter onto the fabric. Remove the paper template once the design is traced. You should be able to reuse it for the other border strips. Repeat for the other three strips.

5. Place the side outer border strips over the side inner borders, right sides up, matching centers and aligning the outer edges of the inner borders with the outer edges of the outer borders. To keep both borders aligned during stitching, pin the borders in place, then baste about ¼" inside the drawn line on the outer border and also along the outer edges.

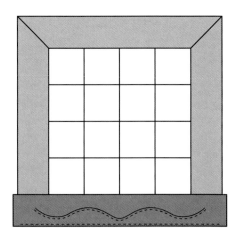

6. Baste the top and bottom outer borders in the same way, with their ends extending beyond the side borders.

7. Beginning approximately 5" from where the miter will be, trim a 5" length of outer border fabric to a ⅛" seam allowance. Head away from the mitered edge as you cut. Be careful not to cut the inner border fabric at the same time!

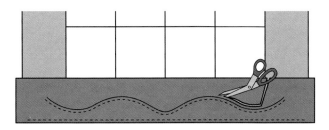

8. Appliqué the outer border to the inner border, turning under the seam allowance with your needle as you go. Turn just a little bit at a time on curves, using a sweeping motion to smooth the seam allowance underneath.

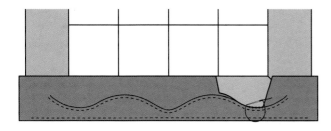

Sew right up to the peak of points, then sweep the other side under with the needle.

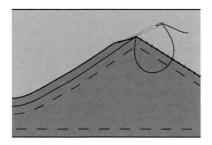

Continue stitching, trimming the seam allowance as you go. Stop several inches from the next miter. Appliqué the remaining outer borders in the same way.

9. Fold the top and bottom outer borders over the sides to make the miters and to finish the corners. You may need to fiddle with them a bit to adjust the miters and make the curves flow smoothly around the corners. Check the miters with a ruler to be sure the 45-degree angle is correct, and trim as needed. Appliqué the corners and miters, sewing only the outer border fabric into the miter.

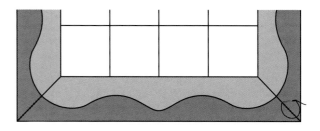

10. When the outer border is completely appliquéd and the miters have been sewn, remove the basting, turn the quilt over, and trim the inner border fabric behind the outer border fabric. Trim the border to within ¼" of the appliquéd edge.

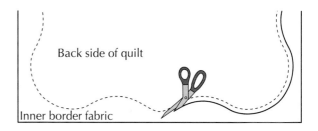

Finishing Techniques

Take a little while to celebrate and enjoy your completed top before you move on to the next steps. Taking a break allows you to savor the pleasure of a completed top and mull over the quilting design. Because I quilt my small quilts by hand, I may spend as much time on the quilting and binding as I do on the piecing and appliqué, so I like to consider carefully how best to finish the quilt. Experience has taught me that if I get in a hurry to be done, I tend to make compromises I'm sorry about later. After a little time off, I can return to the quilt with a fresh outlook, ready to give the final steps of the process the time and attention they deserve.

THE QUILTING DESIGN

Before layering the quilt with batting and backing, you need to decide how you will quilt it. If your quilt plan includes an elaborate design such as cables or feathers, you may want to mark the quilting design on the top before basting. It's easier to mark accurately while the top is perfectly flat, and you can often use a light box to trace the design, which eliminates the need for stencils. For a small quilt, it's easy to draw the entire design—corners and all—on paper, and trace it directly onto the top. If your quilt plan is simple, like outline or straight line quilting, you can mark as you go. Don't forget to test your marking tool to be sure it can be removed!

Each quilt pattern in this book includes a suggested quilting plan. Most of the plans are simple, chosen to enhance the appliquéd and pieced patterns rather than to be strong design elements. Quilting "in the ditch" around each appliqué piece defines the pieces, making them stand out more. Quilting a filler pattern, such as diagonal lines or crosshatching, in the surrounding background further enhances the appliqué.

BACKING AND BATTING

Choose backing fabric that complements the front of the quilt and the binding. If the front of the quilt is very light, choose backing that won't shadow through the batting.

Cut the backing and the batting at least 1" larger than the quilt on all sides. I sometimes cut the backing generously so the excess fabric will hold the hoop when I'm quilting the borders. Wasteful, I know, but sometimes the time saved by not having to add strips for the hoop is worth it!

Small quilts call for thin batting. A thick batting can make a small quilt look bunchy and overstuffed. For years, I split batting to get the desired thinness, but happily there are now many suitable battings available. Polyester is the easiest to needle and is a good choice for hand quilting. I use the thinnest I can find. Soft and thin cotton battings that give good results are available as well. While cotton is often harder to needle than polyester, it gives a flatter, more old-fashioned look that makes it worth the extra effort for special quilts. Use good-quality batting that folds and drapes nicely. Many lovely quilts have been ruined by "bargain batting." Too much time and love go into making the top to compromise on what's inside.

BASTING AND QUILTING

I prefer to baste my small quilts by hand with needle and thread. A small quilt doesn't take long to baste, and basting keeps the layers from shifting during quilting.

Working on a flat surface, layer the backing, wrong side up, with the batting and then the top. Baste through all layers, beginning in the center and working out in each direction, making sure to keep the layers smooth. Baste a line approximately every 3" in each direction in a grid pattern, and then all around the outside edge.

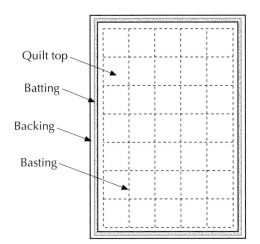

Quilt top

Batting

Backing

Basting

Begin quilting in the center of the quilt. Work out from the center in each direction, smoothing the layers as you go. Avoid skipping around, which can result in unwanted puckers and bumps.

I like to quilt with a hoop. I can quilt without one, but it is never my "Sunday best" quilting. Set the hoop on the quilt gently to avoid pulling at the points of tiny appliqués. If there isn't enough fabric to secure the edge of the quilt to the hoop, baste a strip of muslin to each side of the quilt top. I use the long basting stitch on my machine for this.

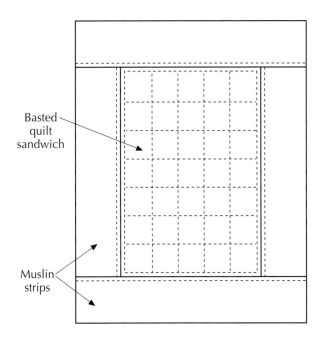

Basted quilt sandwich

Muslin strips

BINDING

Straight, even binding with tidy corners helps a quilt finish flat and square. For a quilt with straight sides and square corners, binding strips can be cut on the straight grain or on the bias. If the edges or corners are curved, the binding strips must be cut on the bias so that they will be flexible enough to follow the curves. Some fabrics, such as stripes or plaids, look better when cut on the bias.

1. Use a rotary cutter to trim the sides of the quilt so all layers are even and the corners are square. Baste the three layers together all around the edge so they won't shift while you apply the binding.

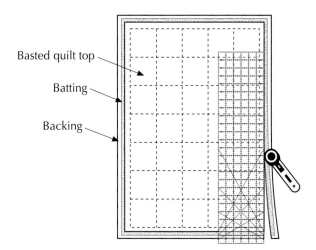

Basted quilt top

Batting

Backing

2. Total the outside dimensions of the quilt (the perimeter) and add 4" to this measurement. This is the length of binding you will need for your quilt. Cut the binding strips 2" wide, either on the straight grain or on the bias. Join the strips with a diagonal seam to reduce bulk, trim the seam allowances to ¼", and press them open.

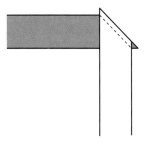

3. Fold the binding in half lengthwise with wrong sides together, and press. Fold under a ¼" seam allowance at one end of the long strip.

Fold line

4. Lay the binding on the front of the quilt, aligning all the raw edges. Place the end of the binding approximately 5" from a corner. Pin, then begin stitching 3" from the end of the binding. (You want to leave an unsewn tail.) Sew with the usual ¼" seam allowance. Stop stitching ¼" from the corner and backstitch.

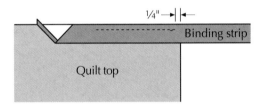
¼"
Binding strip
Quilt top

5. Fold the binding diagonally so that it is perpendicular to the edge you just stitched.

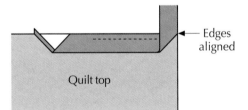
Edges aligned
Quilt top

6. Fold the binding straight down so the fold is even with the edge of the quilt. If the fold extends beyond the edge, the corner will not be square. Start sewing at the folded edge, backstitching at the beginning. Continue stitching around the quilt until you are 3" from the starting point.

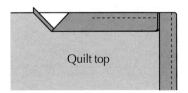
Quilt top

7. Trim the end of the binding so it overlaps the beginning by 2". Tuck the cut end of the binding strip inside the diagonal fold. Be sure that the join is smooth on the long folded edge. Pin, then finish sewing the binding to the quilt.

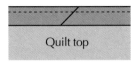
Quilt top

To keep the layers from shifting while you stitch, use a walking foot when applying the binding. This special presser foot "walks" over the top layer of fabric as you stitch, allowing multiple layers to feed through the machine at the same rate.

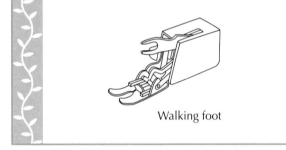
Walking foot

8. Fold the binding over the edge of the quilt and hand stitch it to the backing, using the appliqué stitch. As you fold each corner back, a miter will form on the front. To make a similar miter on the back, fold down one side of the binding, then the other. Finish the binding by hand, stitching the diagonal folds of the miters and the diagonal seam where the binding ends.

Quilt back   Quilt back

Animal Crackers

by Elizabeth Hamby Carlson, 1995, Montgomery Village, Maryland, 19" × 25". Colorful animal appliqués, drawn from a collection of old cookie cutters, inhabit pieced blocks in this cheerful quilt.

Christmas Cookies

by Elizabeth Hamby Carlson, 1995, Montgomery Village, Maryland, 20¼" × 20¼". A traditional pieced pattern surrounds Christmas cookie appliqués to make a festive quilt.

Roses of Lancaster

by Elizabeth Hamby Carlson, 1991, Montgomery Village, Maryland, 17" × 17". Pastel colors, traditional Lancaster Rose blocks, and a scalloped swag border combine to create an appealing design.

Grandmother's Trellis Garden

by Elizabeth Hamby Carlson, 1994, Montgomery Village, Maryland, 28" × 36". Pieced Trellis blocks surround colorful hexagon flowers blooming fresh as a summer's day.

Trellis Garden II

by Elizabeth Hamby Carlson, 1994, Montgomery Village, Maryland, 15½" × 20". A simple flower appliqué replaces the hexagon rosette on this "little sister" of "Grandmother's Trellis Garden."

School Days

by Elizabeth Hamby Carlson, 1992, Montgomery Village, Maryland, 17" × 24". Tiny appliquéd apples and pieced Schoolhouse blocks make a quilt that would delight any teacher.

Bountiful Harvest

by Elizabeth Hamby Carlson, 1992, Montgomery Village, Maryland, 21" × 21". Reminiscent of a mid–nineteenth-century Album quilt, this colorful design features the fruits of the harvest. Snappy sawtooth borders add a festive finishing touch.

Autumn Flight

by Elizabeth Hamby Carlson, 1992, Montgomery Village, Maryland, 21" × 24". Scrappy strips of Flying Geese and a border of colorful leaves lend this quilt its autumnal air.

Irish Rose

by Elizabeth Hamby Carlson, 1998, Montgomery Village, Maryland, 26¼" × 26¼". Two old favorites, the Irish Chain and the Rose of Sharon, combine in a red and green quilt perfect for the holidays, or for any time.

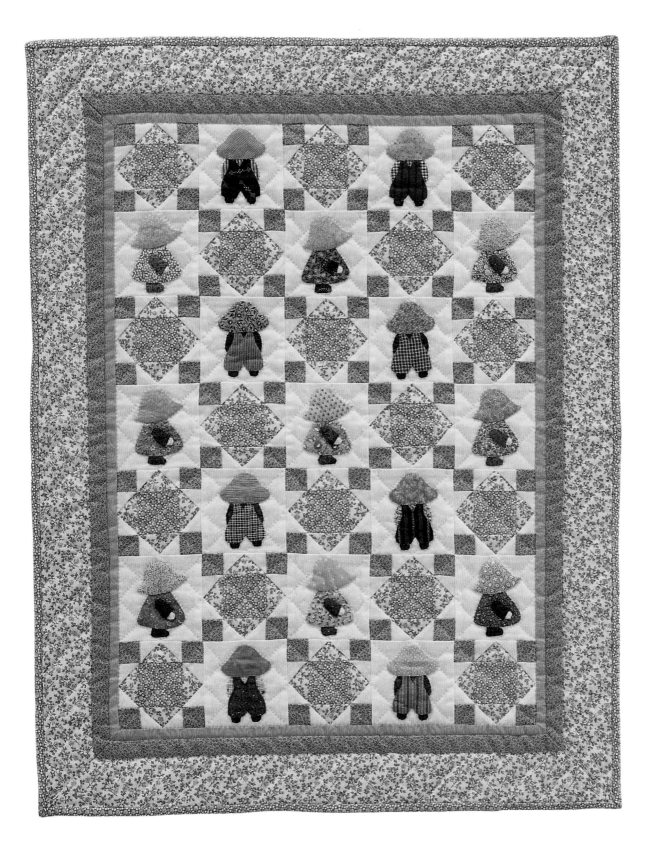

Sunbonnet Friends

by Elizabeth Hamby Carlson, 1998, Montgomery Village, Maryland, 21" × 26½". Those perennial favorites, Sunbonnet Sue and Overall Sam, enliven this scaled-down version of my first quilt.

Teapot Traditions

by Elizabeth Hamby Carlson, 1995, Montgomery Village, Maryland, 17" × 17". A graceful scalloped border complements this cupboard full of appliquéd teapots, inspired by designs from eighteenth- and early nineteenth-century England.

Bridal Wreath

by Elizabeth Hamby Carlson, 1998, Montgomery Village, Maryland, 35" × 35". Winding vines and hearts frame Bridal Wreath blocks to create a pretty quilt fashioned with reproduction fabrics.

40 ∾

Animal Crackers

A collection of old cookie cutters inspired this cheerful quilt, just right for tucking in a chair with a favorite stuffed animal. The piecing is simple and quick, the appliquéd animals are fun, and a second, darker background fabric makes a built-in border to frame it all.

> ❧ Think of the medium-value background as a border fabric. The fabrics you select for the blocks and the appliqués should contrast sharply with both background fabrics. Using lots of different prints will make your quilt scrappier and more interesting. I chose nineteenth-century reproduction prints to lend my quilt an old-fashioned flavor. Bright primary colors would give a cheerful, contemporary look.

Quilt Size: 19" × 25½"
Finished Block Size: 4½"

Materials: 42"-wide fabric

½ yd. light for background
⅔ yd. medium for background
⅓ yd. *total* assorted mediums and darks for blocks
   and appliqués
¾ yd. for backing
¼ yd. dark for binding
21" × 27½" piece of batting

Cutting

All measurements include ¼"-wide seam allowances.

From the light background fabric, cut:

48 squares, each 1¼", for blocks
24 squares, each 2", for blocks
6 oversize squares, each 6", for appliqué backgrounds

From the medium background fabric, cut:

48 squares, each 1¼", for blocks
24 squares, each 2", for blocks
3 squares, each 7⅝", for side setting triangles
2 squares, each 4⅛", for corner setting triangles

From the assorted medium and dark fabrics, cut a total of:

4 squares, each 2", for blocks
96 squares, each 1¼", for blocks

Pieced Blocks

The pieced blocks are all constructed in the same manner, but there are three different arrangements of background fabric, depending on where the block appears in the quilt. The blocks in the center use only the light background, while the side and corner blocks use different combinations of both background fabrics. Lay out the pieced blocks on a design wall to arrange the colors and to be sure you are placing the background fabrics correctly.

See "Piecing with Precision" on pages 20–24 for general construction techniques. You'll need to make a total of 12 pieced blocks in the combinations shown.

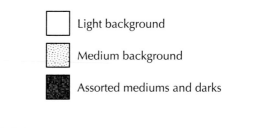

☐ Light background

▨ Medium background

■ Assorted mediums and darks

Center Block
Make 2.
   Side Block
Make 6.
   Corner Block
Make 4.

1. For each block, make 4 four-patch units as shown, using 1¼" squares. Each four-patch unit should measure 2" square. Press the seam allowances as indicated by the arrows.

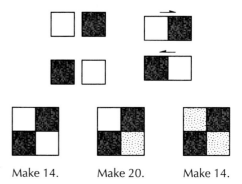

Make 14.   Make 20.   Make 14.

2. Assemble each pieced block using 4 four-patch units, four 2" background squares, and one 2" dark or medium square for each block. Press the seam allowances as indicated by the arrows.

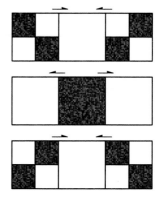

Appliquéd Blocks

See "Appliquéing Small Quilts" on pages 11–19 for general appliqué techniques.

1. Fold each 6" background square in quarters to find its center, then crease the block on both diagonals.

2. Fold a sheet of freezer paper in half. Using the templates on page 44, trace 2 of each animal shape onto the folded paper, then cut out the shapes. Because of the fold, you'll have 4 templates of each shape, 2 of which will be reversed.

3. Press each freezer-paper template to the wrong side of the appropriate appliqué fabric. Cut out the animal shapes, adding a ³⁄₁₆" seam allowance all around, and baste the seams as desired. Keeping like animals together, arrange 4 on each block as shown in the photo on page 33.

4. Pin or baste the appliqués in place, keeping them within the 4½" finished size of the background blocks. Appliqué the pieces to the blocks, then remove the paper templates (see "Removing the Glue and Freezer Paper" on pages 18–19).

5. Square up and trim the completed appliqué blocks to measure 5" (see "Squaring Up the Blocks" on page 25).

Note: *Be sure to measure your work.* The dimensions of the appliqué blocks must match the dimensions of the pieced blocks.

Quilt Assembly

1. Cut each 7⅝" medium background square in half twice diagonally to make 10 side setting triangles with the straight grain on the long side. There will be 2 extra triangles.

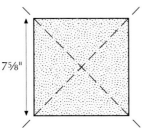

2. Cut each 4⅛" medium background square in half once diagonally to make 4 corner setting triangles. Each square yields 2 corner triangles with the straight grain on the short sides.

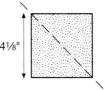

3. Arrange the blocks and setting triangles as shown in the quilt photo. Make sure the block placement is correct. It's easy to mistakenly turn a block the wrong way!

4. Sew the blocks together in diagonal rows, finishing each row with the appropriate side triangle. Press all seam allowances toward the pieced blocks. Pin and sew the diagonal rows together, adding the corner triangles last. Square-up the quilt-top corners as necessary.

5. Machine stitch ³⁄₁₆" from the raw edge all around the quilt top to prevent it from stretching while you quilt.

Finishing

See "Finishing Techniques" on pages 30–32.

1. Mark the quilt top for quilting according to the quilting plan or as desired.
2. Layer the quilt top with the backing and batting; baste and quilt.
3. Trim the edges of the backing and batting even with the quilt top. Bind the edges.

Quilting Plan

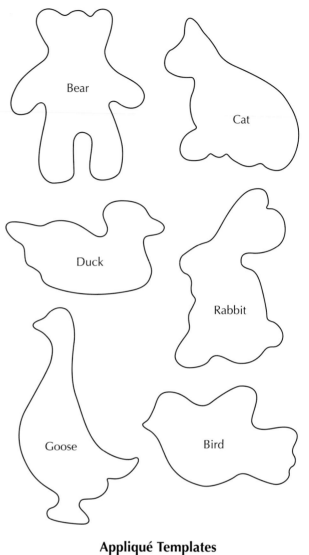

Appliqué Templates
Cut 2 and 2 reversed of each template.

Christmas Cookies

What could be more festive than a platter full of gaily decorated Christmas cookies? Why, a quilt full of Christmas cookies, of course! These colorful cookies will last through many holidays to come, and they really are fat-free! It's so easy to piece and appliqué, you'll have this little gem ready for Christmas even if you finish the Thanksgiving turkey before you start.

🍂 *Three different background fabrics help to give "Christmas Cookies" the look of a medallion set. Choose the background fabrics carefully by auditioning options on a design wall. Select fabrics that contrast sharply with the backgrounds. Reds and greens will give your quilt a seasonal look, while hints of gold—particularly in the backgrounds—will make it glow.*

Quilt Size: 20¼" × 20¼"

Materials: 42"-wide fabric

⅜ yd. light for blocks and appliqué backgrounds
(background 1)

⅛ yd. medium beige for blocks (background 2)

½ yd. medium red for blocks, appliqué backgrounds,
and corner squares (background 3)

½ yd. *total* assorted mediums and darks for blocks
and appliqués

⅔ yd. for backing

¼ yd. dark for binding

22¼" × 22¼" piece of batting

Cutting

All measurements include ¼"-wide seam allowances.

From the light fabric (background 1), cut:
60 squares, each 1¼", for blocks
4 oversize rectangles, each 3¾" × 8¼", for appliqué
backgrounds

From the medium beige fabric (background 2), cut:
12 squares, each 1¼", for blocks

From the medium red fabric (background 3), cut:
92 squares, each 1¼", for blocks
12 squares, each 2¾", for corner squares
8 oversize squares, each 3¾", for appliqué backgrounds
4 oversize rectangles, each 3¾" × 8¼", for
appliqué backgrounds

**From the assorted medium and dark fabrics, cut
a total of:**
169 squares, each 1¼", for blocks

Pieced Blocks

Before you stitch, lay out the quilt on a design
wall to arrange the colors and to be sure you are
placing the background fabrics correctly. Some
pieced blocks use more than one background fabric.

See "Piecing with Precision" on pages 20–24
for general construction techniques. When making

rows for pieced units, press all seam allowances
toward the darker fabric.

1. Use 1¼" squares to assemble the center square.
   Sew 9 rows of 9 squares each, and press.
   Pinning carefully, sew the rows together. Press
   the seam allowances away from the center of
   the square as indicated by the arrows.

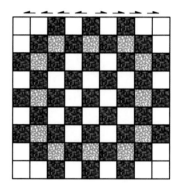

2. Use 1¼" squares to assemble 4 pieced rectangles as shown. For each rectangle, sew 3 rows of
   9 squares each. Pinning carefully, sew the rows
   together. Press the seam allowances away from
   the center row.

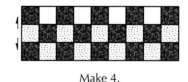

Make 4.

3. Use 1¼" squares to assemble 16 nine-patch
   units as shown. For each unit, sew 3 rows of 3
   squares each. Pinning carefully, sew the rows
   together. Press the seam allowances away from
   the center row.

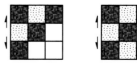

Make 4.   Make 12.

Appliquéd Blocks

See "Appliquéing Small Quilts" on pages 11–19 for general appliqué techniques.

1. Fold each 3¾" × 8¼" background rectangle in half lengthwise and crosswise to find the center point, and lightly crease the folds.
2. Using the templates on page 48, make 3 freezer-paper templates for each cookie shape.

Note: The candle, candy cane, and stocking are asymmetrical shapes. You will need to make reverse templates to cut these 3 appliqués. See "Making Freezer-Paper Templates" on pages 14–15. All the other appliqués in this quilt are symmetrical and may be traced and cut in the usual fashion.

3. Press each freezer-paper template to the wrong side of the appropriate appliqué fabric. Cut out the shapes, adding a ³⁄₁₆" seam allowance all around, and baste the seams as desired.
4. Arrange 3 like cookie shapes on each background rectangle, keeping the appliqués within the 2¼" × 6¾" finished size of the block. Use the photo on page 34 as a guide. Appliqué the center shapes first, then appliqué one shape on each side. Remove the paper templates (see "Removing the Glue and Freezer Paper" on page 18).
5. Fold each 3¾" medium red square in quarters to find its center point, then crease the block on both diagonals.
6. Using the templates on page 48, make 16 freezer-paper templates for holly leaves and 8 for holly berries.
7. Press each freezer-paper template to the wrong side of the appropriate appliqué fabric. Cut out the leaves and berries, adding a ³⁄₁₆" seam allowance all around, and baste the seams as desired. Appliqué the holly to the 3¾" squares, keeping within the 2¼" finished size of the block. Remove the paper templates.

8. Trim and square up the appliquéd rectangles to measure 2¾" × 7¼", and the appliquéd squares to measure 2¾". (See "Squaring Up the Blocks" on page 25.)

Note: *Be sure to measure your work. The dimensions of the appliqué blocks must match the dimensions of the pieced blocks.*

Quilt Assembly

1. Referring to the quilt photo, arrange the blocks and the medium red corner squares, making sure they are positioned correctly.
2. Sew the blocks together in horizontal rows. Press the seam allowances toward the plain or appliquéd blocks. Pin and sew the rows together to complete the quilt top.

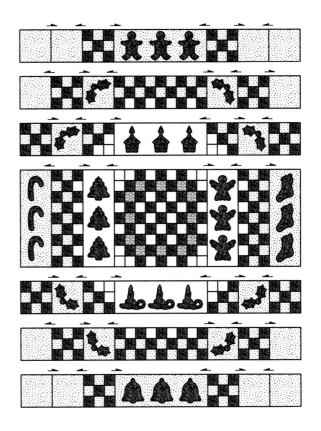

3. Using your sewing machine, staystitch ³⁄₁₆" from the raw edge all around the quilt top to prevent it from stretching while you quilt.

Finishing

See "Finishing Techniques" on pages 30–32.

1. Mark the quilt top for quilting according to the quilting plan or as desired.
2. Layer the quilt top with the backing and batting; baste and quilt.
3. Trim the edges of the backing and batting even with the quilt top. Bind the edges.

Quilting Plan

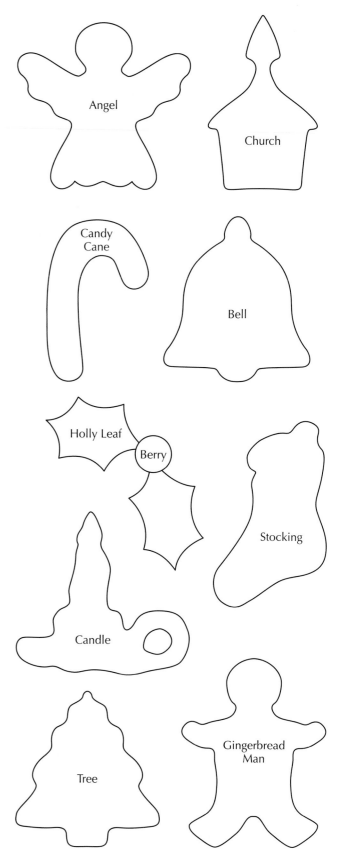

Appliqué Templates
Cut candle, candy cane, and stocking in reverse.

Roses of Lancaster

This quilt combines some of my favorite things: traditional Lancaster Rose blocks, a scalloped swag border, and pretty, feminine colors. The first version I made was raffled in my quilt guild's silent auction. I liked it so much I didn't mind making another, and eight years later it is still one of my favorites. It can usually be found in my living room, tucked into my childhood rocking chair around my daughter Kate's china doll.

Pastel colors and soft—but still distinct—contrasts give my quilt a gentle, feminine look. I used only medium and light values, no true darks, relying on color contrast as much as value contrast to define the pieces. A low-contrast background print (rather than a solid) further softens the look. The narrow sashing strips are quite thin, so be sure they will show up next to the wider strips. For the wide sashing strips, slender stripes can be very effective. Holiday reds and greens would make a festive quilt with a completely different look, and hand-dyed fabrics would also work well.

Quilt Size: 17" × 17"
Finished Block Size: 4"

Materials: 42"-wide fabric

½ yd. light for appliqué background and borders

¼ yd. light blue stripe for wide sashing strips

⅜ yd. medium pink for Template #2, narrow sashing strips, and binding

¼ yd. medium-dark blue for corner squares and swags (Templates #7 and #8)

⅛ yd. light pink for Template #3

⅛ yd. medium green for Template #1

⅛ yd. medium blue for Template #6

6" light blue square or scraps for Template #4

6" dark blue square or scraps for Template #5

⅝ yd. fabric for backing

19" × 19" piece of batting

Cutting

All measurements include ¼"-wide seam allowances.

From the light fabric, cut:

4 oversize squares, each 5½", for appliqué backgrounds

4 strips, each 4¼" × 18", for borders

From the light blue stripe fabric, cut:

12 strips, each 1⅛" × 4½", for wide sashing

From the medium pink fabric, cut:

24 strips, each 11⁄16" × 4½", for narrow sashing

From the medium-dark blue fabric, cut:

9 squares, each 1½", for corner squares

Note: The finished width of the sashing unit is 1". You can alter the width of the narrow and wide sashing strips (or eliminate the narrow strips entirely), as long as the finished width of the sashing unit is still 1". Keep this option in mind when auditioning stripes for the sashing units. If you find the perfect 1" stripe, by all means use it!

Appliquéd Blocks

See "Appliquéing Small Quilts" on pages 11–19 for general appliqué techniques.

1. Fold each 5½" background square in quarters to find its center point, then crease the block on both diagonals. Referring to "Preparing Background Fabric" on page 13, prepare the squares for appliqué. Use the appliqué placement diagram on page 52 as a guide.

2. Using the templates on page 52, make 16 freezer-paper templates each of Templates #1, #2, #3, and #6. Make 4 templates each for Templates #4 and #5. Because these blocks are small and symmetrical, it is especially important that the freezer-paper templates be accurate. Make a plastic half-template of each shape first, then cut the paper on the fold (see "Making Freezer-Paper Templates" on pages 14–15).

3. Press the freezer-paper templates to the wrong side of the appropriate appliqué fabrics. Cut out the fabric shapes, adding a 3⁄16" seam allowance all around. Leave an extra-wide seam allowance on the straight edges of piece 6. Those edges will form the outer corners of the block and will be trimmed when you square up the block.

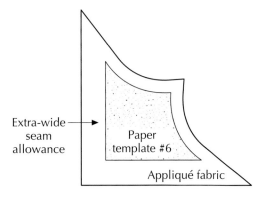

4. Pin, then appliqué the pieces to the background blocks in numerical order, keeping them within the 4" finished size of the blocks. Do not turn under the straight edges of piece 6, as they will be sewn into the seam when the blocks are joined. Remove the paper templates (see "Removing the Glue and Freezer Paper" on pages 18–19).

5. Trim and square up the completed blocks to measure 4½" (see "Squaring Up the Blocks" on page 25).

Assembling the Quilt

1. Make 12 sashing units by sewing a narrow sashing strip to the long edges of each wide sashing strip. Trim the seam allowances to ⅛" and press them toward the narrow strips.

Sashing unit

2. Arrange the blocks, sashing units, and corner squares in rows as shown. Sew the pieces into rows, pressing the seam allowances toward the sashing strips. Pinning carefully, sew the rows together, pressing the seams away from the appliqué blocks.

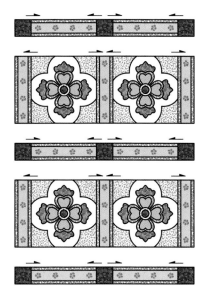

Borders

1. Sew a light border strip to each side of the quilt, mitering the corners (see "Mitered Borders" on pages 26–27).
2. Make 4 freezer-paper templates of Template #8, 12 of Template #7, and 16 of Template #2.
3. Press the freezer-paper templates to the wrong side of the appropriate appliqué fabrics. Cut out the fabric shapes, adding a ³⁄₁₆" seam allowance and a little extra on the short ends

of pieces 7 and 8. This extra fabric allows you to make any necessary adjustments when placing the swags around the border.

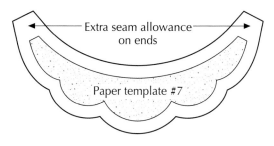

Paper template #7

4. Use the border placement diagram to arrange the swags and hearts around the 4 sides of the border, keeping in mind that the borders can be trimmed a bit. Pin or baste, then sew the appliqués in place. Remove the paper templates.

Finishing

See "Finishing Techniques" on pages 30–32.
1. Mark the quilt top for quilting according to the quilting plan or as desired.
2. Layer the quilt top with the backing and batting; baste and quilt.
3. When the quilting is complete, trim the quilt top, backing, and batting to measure 17" × 17". Bind the edges.

Quilting Plan

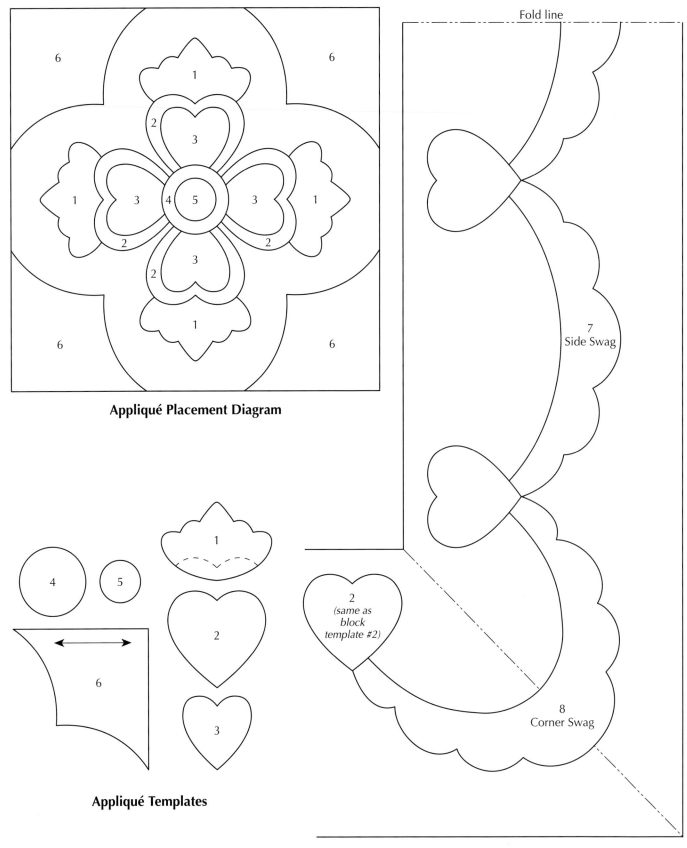

Appliqué Placement Diagram

Appliqué Templates

Border Placement Diagram and Templates

Grandmother's Trellis Garden

A UFO (unfinished object) provided the inspiration for this quilt. After taking a class to make a tiny Grandmother's Flower Garden quilt, I eagerly made a dozen hexagon rosettes, then set them aside to work on something else. A year or two later, I came across the rosettes while cleaning my work room. By that time, it was clear the quilt I had originally planned was a fantasy. I knew I would never piece the hundreds more tiny hexagons I needed. Still, those rosettes were awfully sweet, and it seemed a shame not to use them in some way. I decided to appliqué them to blocks that would alternate with piecework, and "Grandmother's Trellis Garden" was born. It's satisfying to have a finished quilt and one less UFO!

The hexagon rosettes are assembled with English paper-piecing, a method that is fun and somewhat addictive. A friend of mine uses it for nearly all her piecing projects. I like it as a change of pace, and as an easy way to get oddly shaped pieces to fit together.

✳ *Here is a quilt for those little, multicolored floral prints that can be hard to use. Floral prints are just right for the rosettes, and I used one for the sashing and borders as well. To make the sashing and pieced block suggest a trellis, keep the value of the sashing fabric close to the value of the strips in the pieced block. If the values contrast too sharply, one element—either the sashing or the pieced block—will overpower the other.*

Quilt Size: 28" × 36"
Finished Block Size: 3½"

Materials: 42"-wide fabric

1⅛ yds. light for appliqué backgrounds, blocks, and inner borders

¼ yd. medium pink print for trellis strips

⅛ yd. medium pink solid for trellis center squares

1⅛ yds. medium green print for sashing, outer border, and binding

⅛ yd. medium green solid for sashing corner squares

⅓ yd. *total* assorted mediums and darks for appliqués

Coordinating scraps for appliqué centers

1⅛ yds. fabric for backing

30" × 38" piece of batting

Cutting

All measurements include ¼"-wide seam allowances.

From the light fabric, cut:

17 oversize squares, each 5", for appliqué backgrounds

18 squares, each 4⅛", for blocks

2 strips, each 4¼" × 28½", for top and bottom inner borders

2 strips, each 4¼" × 36½", for side inner borders

From the medium pink print, cut:

72 strips, each 1" × 3", for trellis (B)

From the medium pink solid, cut:

18 squares, each 1", for trellis center squares (C)

From the medium green print, cut:

82 strips, each 1" × 4", for sashing strips

2 strips, each 4" × 29", for top and bottom outer borders

2 strips, each 4" × 37", for side outer borders

From the medium green solid, cut:

48 squares, each 1", for sashing corner squares

Pieced Blocks

See "Piecing with Precision" on pages 20–24 for general construction techniques. Because the trellis and sashing strips are so narrow, take extra care to sew accurately and to trim the seam allowances to ⅛".

1. Cut each 4⅛" light square in half twice diagonally, so that each square yields 4 triangles (A) with the straight grain on the long side. There will be a total of 72 triangles.

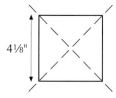

2. Arrange 4 triangles (A) with 4 pink trellis strips (B) and a pink solid center square (C). Sew the pieces into rows as shown. Press all seam allowances toward the trellis fabric.

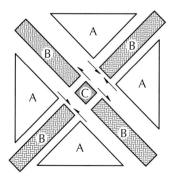

3. Sew the rows together and press the seam allowances toward the center row. The trellis strips will extend beyond the block corners.

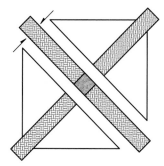

4. Repeat steps 2 and 3 to make a total of 18 blocks. Use a rotary cutter and Bias Square ruler to square up and trim each block to 4".

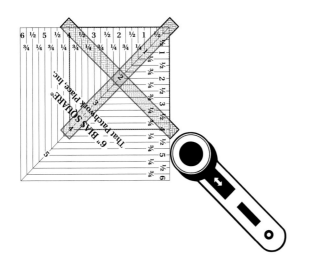

Appliquéd Blocks

See "Appliquéing Small Quilts" on pages 11–19 for general appliqué techniques.

1. Make plastic templates of hexagon Templates #1 and #2 (page 57). To ensure accuracy, cut the template plastic with a utility knife and straight-edge rather than with scissors.

2. Trace around Template #1 on the *right* side of the appliqué fabrics. Cut hexagons for 17 rosettes. Each rosette uses 2 fabrics, one for the 6 petals and one for the center. Cut out the hexagons right on the lines.

3. Use Template #2 to make 119 freezer-paper templates. Center a paper template, shiny side down, on the *wrong* side of each fabric hexagon and press in place with a hot, dry iron.

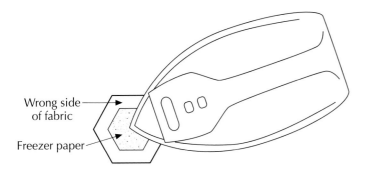

Wrong side of fabric

Freezer paper

4. Fold the seam allowance over each paper hexagon and baste in place. Fold one side at a time to keep the corners crisp.

5. Place the right sides of 2 hexagons together and join them with tiny whipstitches from the wrong side, catching just a few threads at the edge of each. Assemble the rosettes from the center out, joining one side of each petal to the center first, then sewing the petal sides together.

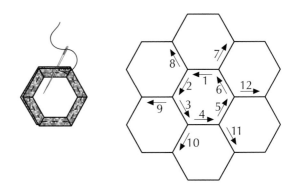

6. Press the rosettes firmly. Carefully remove the basting threads and papers.

7. Fold each 5" background square in quarters to find its center point, then crease the block on both diagonals. Center a rosette on each background square and baste it in place. Appliqué the edges of the rosette to the background. Trim the background fabric behind the rosette if desired.

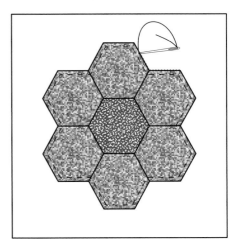

8. Trim and square up the completed blocks to measure 4" (see "Squaring Up the Blocks" on page 25).

Assembling the Quilt

Arrange the blocks, sashing strips, and sashing corner squares in rows as shown. Alternate the pieced and appliquéd blocks, placing a pieced block at each corner of the quilt. Sew the units into rows, pressing all the seam allowances toward the sashing strips. Pin, then sew the rows together, again pressing the seam allowances toward the sashing strips.

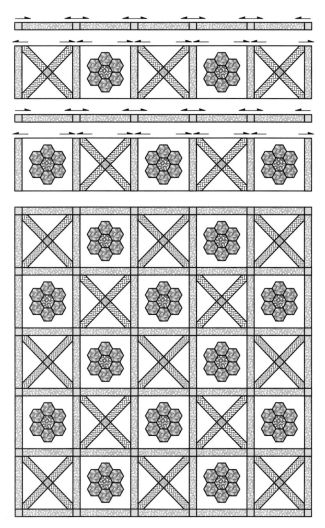

Assembly Diagram

Borders

"Grandmother's Trellis Garden" has zigzagging cutwork borders. See "Cutwork Appliqué Borders" on pages 27–29 for general instructions.

1. Sew the light inner borders to the quilt, mitering the corners (see "Mitered Borders" on pages 26–27).
2. Baste, trim, and appliqué the cutwork borders, using the border template on page 57.

Finishing

See "Finishing Techniques" on pages 30–32.

1. Mark the quilt top for quilting according to the quilting plan or as desired.
2. Layer the quilt top with the backing and batting; baste and quilt.
3. Trim the edges of the backing and batting even with the quilt top. Bind the edges.

Quilting Plan

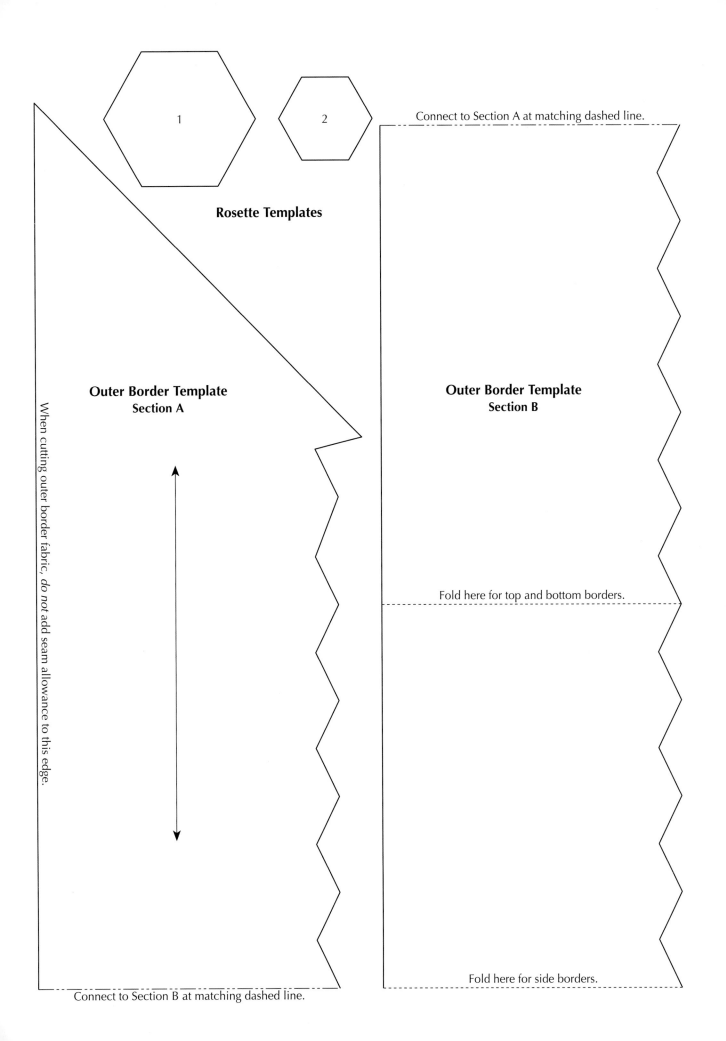

Rosette Templates

1

2

Outer Border Template
Section A

Outer Border Template
Section B

When cutting outer border fabric, *do not* add seam allowance to this edge.

Connect to Section A at matching dashed line.

Fold here for top and bottom borders.

Connect to Section B at matching dashed line.

Fold here for side borders.

Trellis Garden II

As I worked on "Grand-mother's Trellis Garden" (page 53), I couldn't help thinking "Wouldn't it be fun to make another one?" I liked the basic set of the quilt and found that making it once just wasn't enough. The next one, I decided, would be smaller and simpler.

"Trellis Garden II" is constructed just like "Grandmother's Trellis Garden," but instead of hexagon rosettes it has simple flower appliqués, no corner squares to piece, and a scalloped border instead of zigzags. Why not make them both and see which one you like best?

Quilt Size: 16" × 20½"
Finished Block Size: 2"

Materials: 42"-wide fabric

⅝ yd. light for appliqué backgrounds, blocks, and inner borders

⅝ yd. medium blue for trellis, outer borders, and binding

¼ yd. medium pink for sashing

Assorted scraps for appliqués

½ yd. or a fat quarter (18" × 22") for backing

18" × 22½" piece of batting

Cutting

All measurements include ¼"-wide seam allowances.

From the light fabric, cut:

17 oversize squares, each 3½", for appliqué backgrounds

18 squares, each 3", for blocks

2 strips, each 2¾" × 16½", for top and bottom inner borders

2 strips, each 2¾" × 21", for side inner borders

From the medium blue fabric, cut:

36 strips, each ¾" × 2", for trellis strips (B)

18 strips, each ¾" × 3⅞", for trellis strips (C)

2 strips, each 2½" × 17", for top and bottom outer borders

2 strips, each 2½" × 21½", for side outer borders

From the medium pink fabric, cut:

30 strips, each ¾" × 2½", for short horizontal sashing

6 strips, each ¾" × 16½", for vertical sashing

2 strips, each ¾" × 12", for long horizontal sashing

Pieced Blocks

See "Piecing with Precision" on pages 20–24 for general construction techniques. Because the trellis and sashing strips are so narrow, take extra care to sew accurately and to trim the seam allowances to ⅛".

1. Cut each 3" light square in half twice diagonally. Each square yields 4 triangles (A) with the straight grain on the long side. There will be a total of 72 triangles.

2. Arrange 4 triangles (A) with 1 long (C) and 2 short (B) blue trellis strips. Sew the pieces into rows as shown, then join the rows. The trellis strips will extend beyond the corners of the block. Press all seam allowances toward the trellis fabric.

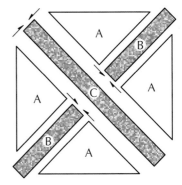

3. Use a rotary cutter and Bias Square to square up and trim each block to measure 2½".

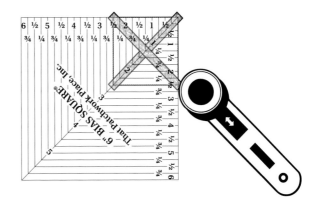

4. Repeat steps 2 and 3 to make a total of 18 pieced blocks.

Appliquéd Blocks

See "Appliquéing Small Quilts" on pages 11–19 for general appliqué techniques.

1. Using the templates on page 61, make 17 flower templates and 17 flower-center templates from freezer paper.

2. Press each freezer-paper template to the wrong side of the appropriate appliqué fabric. Cut out the fabric shapes, adding a ³⁄₁₆" seam allowance all around, and baste the seams as desired.

3. Fold each 3½" background square in quarters to find its center point, then crease the block on both diagonals. Center, baste, and appliqué first a flower, then a flower center, to each background block. Remove the paper templates (see "Removing the Glue and Freezer Paper" on pages 18–19). Make 17 Flower blocks.

4. Trim and square up the blocks to measure 2½" (see "Squaring Up the Blocks" on page 25).

Assembling the Quilt

Arrange the blocks and the sashing strips, alternating pieced and appliquéd blocks as shown. Sew the blocks and short sashing strips in 5 vertical rows, then join the rows with the long vertical sashing strips. Finish by adding the long horizontal sashing strips to the top and bottom edges of the quilt top.

Borders

"Trellis Garden II" has scalloped cutwork borders. See "Cutwork Appliqué Borders" on pages 27–29 for general construction techniques.

1. Sew the light inner borders to the quilt, mitering the corners (see "Mitered Borders" on pages 26–27).

2. Baste, trim, and appliqué the cutwork borders, using the border template on page 61.

Finishing

See "Finishing Techniques" on pages 30–32.

1. Mark the quilt top for quilting according to the quilting plan or as desired.

2. Layer the quilt top with the backing and batting; baste and quilt.

3. Trim the edges of the backing and batting even with the quilt top. Bind the edges.

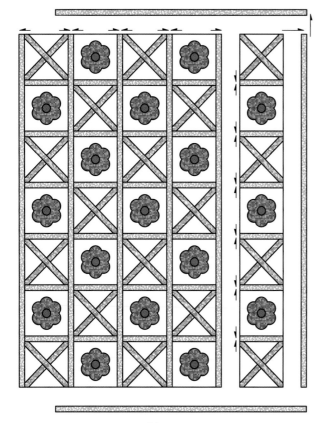

Assembly Diagram

Quilting Plan

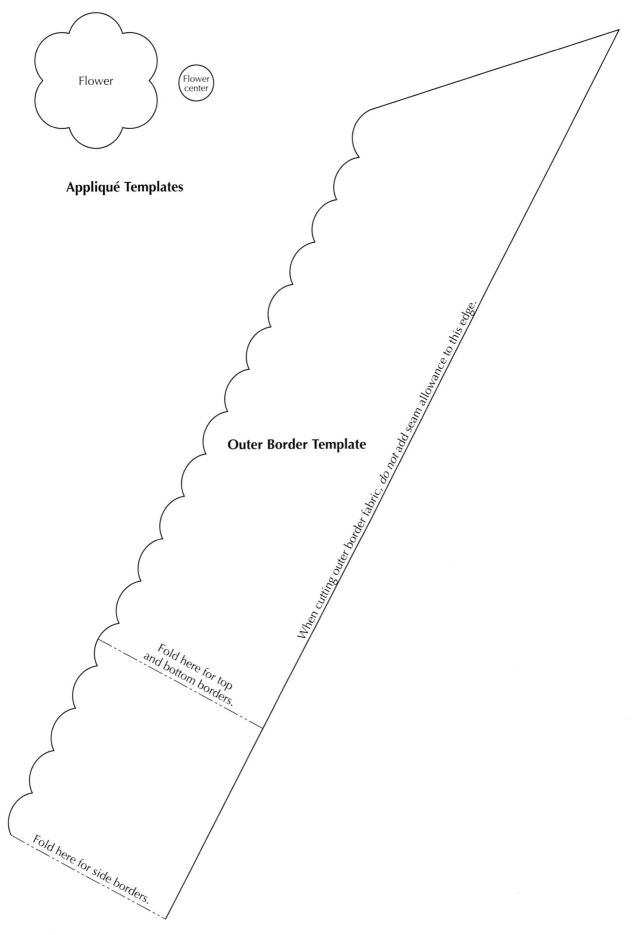

Appliqué Templates

Flower

Flower center

Outer Border Template

When cutting outer border fabric, do not add seam allowance to this edge.

Fold here for top and bottom borders.

Fold here for side borders.

School Days

When my children were young, late August days were filled with back-to-school plans. As we shopped for notebooks and crayons, I thought about making a back-to-school quilt. At that busy time, there were always many things to do, and somehow I never quite got to making my quilt. Years went by, and the children grew to be teenagers, no longer excited by new crayons. Yet I still longed to make my tiny "school days" quilt, so I did! Schoolhouse quilts are perennially popular. They have a simple charm that is irresistible to traditional quiltmakers, and as I learned when I finally got started, they are just plain fun to make. I can't imagine why it took me so long.

This primitive pattern called for country colors and fabrics. While it would be faster to make all the houses from the same fabric, the quilt has a more charming, scrappy look when different fabrics are used. Vary the scales and values of the fabrics, as well as the colors. Choose fabrics with dense patterns rather than those with widely spaced motifs so the houses won't look spotty. I made a few more houses than were required—they don't take long, and the leftovers make nice pincushions. Then I auditioned them on my design wall to decide on a pleasing, balanced arrangement.

Quilt Size: 18¼" × 25¼"
Finished Block Size: 3½"

Materials: 42"-wide fabric

½ yd. light for appliqué backgrounds and blocks

¼ yd. *each* of 8 different red and blue prints for schoolhouses

¾ yd. blue plaid for inner and outer borders and binding

⅛ yd. bright red for accent border

⅛ yd. *total* assorted red scraps for apple appliqués

⅛ yd. *total* assorted green scraps for leaf appliqués

¾ yd. fabric for backing

20" × 27" piece of batting

Cutting

All measurements include ¼"-wide seam allowances. Use the templates on page 65.

From the light fabric, cut:

8 rectangles, each 1" × 2", for blocks (A)

16 rectangles, each ⅞" × 1⅝", for blocks (B)

8 squares, each 1⅝", for blocks (F)

24 rectangles, each ⅞" × 1¼", for blocks (H)

16 rectangles, each ¾" × 3½", for blocks (I)

16 rectangles, each ¾" × 4", for blocks (J)

7 oversize squares, each 5", for appliqué backgrounds

From *each* red and blue schoolhouse print, cut:

2 rectangles, each 1" × 2", for blocks (A)

2 rectangles, each ⅞" × 1⅝", for blocks (B)

3 rectangles, each ⅞" × 2", for blocks (C)

1 Template D for blocks*

1 Template E for blocks*

2 squares, each ⅞", for blocks (G)

From the blue plaid fabric, cut:

2 strips, each ⅞" × 19", for top and bottom inner borders

2 strips, each ⅞" × 26", for side inner borders

2 strips, each 3½" × 19", for top and bottom outer borders

2 strips, each 3½" × 26", for side outer borders

From the bright red fabric, cut:

2 strips, each 1" × 19", for top and bottom accent borders

2 strips, each 1" × 26", for side accent borders

*When cutting pieces D and E, place the templates on the right side of the fabric.

Pieced Blocks

Before beginning to sew, refer to the block assembly diagram below and lay out all the pieces for one block so you can see how it is assembled. Stack and label like pieces so you can keep track of them. Trim seam allowances to ⅛" as you go to reduce bulk, and press the seam allowances toward the darker fabrics whenever possible.

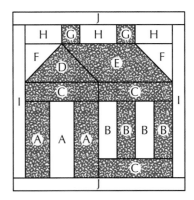

Block Assembly Diagram

1. Sew 2 house strips (A) to a light strip (A) as shown. Sew a house strip (C) to the top edge to complete the doorway unit.

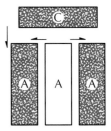

2. Sew 2 light strips (B) to 2 house strips (B) as shown. Sew a house strip (C) to the top and bottom edges to complete the window unit.

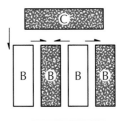

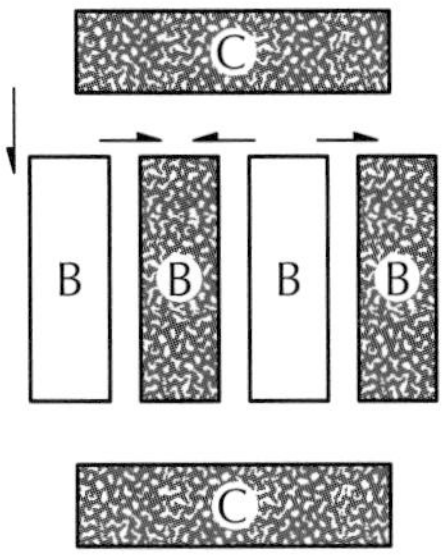

3. Cut a 1⅝" light square in half once diagonally to form 2 triangles (F). Join 2 triangles (F), a house triangle (D), and house piece (E) as shown to make a roof unit.

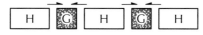

4. Join 3 light strips (H) and 2 house strips (G) as shown to make a chimney unit.

5. Referring to the block assembly diagram, sew the units together. Sew background strips (I) to the sides, then sew a background strip (J) to the top and bottom edges. Press the seams toward the house.

6. Repeat steps 1–5 to make a total of 8 Schoolhouse blocks.

Appliquéd Blocks

See "Appliquéing Small Quilts" on pages 11–19 for general appliqué techniques.

1. Fold each 5" light square in quarters to find its center point, then crease the block on both diagonals. Referring to "Preparing Background Fabric" on page 13, prepare the squares for appliqué. Use the appliqué placement diagram on page 65 as a guide.

2. Cut 35 apple templates and 35 leaf templates from freezer paper.

3. Press each freezer-paper template to the wrong side of the appropriate appliqué fabric. Cut out the fabric shapes, adding 3⁄16" seam allowances all around, and baste the seams as desired.

4. Pin and appliqué the apples, then the leaves, to the background blocks. Be sure to keep the appliqués within the 3½" finished size of the

background block. Remove the paper templates (see "Removing the Glue and Freezer Paper" on pages 18–19).

5. Add a stem to each apple with a brown, fine-line permanent pen.

6. Square up the blocks to measure 4" (see "Squaring Up the Blocks" on page 25).

Assembling the Quilt

Arrange the blocks in 5 horizontal rows of 3 blocks each. Alternate the pieced and appliquéd blocks, beginning with a pieced block at each corner. Sew the blocks into rows, pressing the seam allowances as indicated by the arrows. Join the rows, pinning carefully, to form the quilt top.

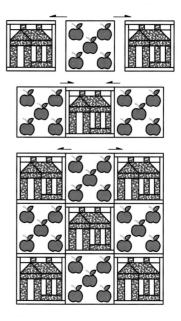

Borders

1. Sew together a ⅞"-wide blue plaid strip, a 1"-wide bright red strip, and a 3½"-wide blue plaid strip, matching lengths, to make a border unit. Make 4 border units: 2 for the sides, and 1 each for the top and bottom of the quilt. Press the seam allowances toward the red fabric.

2. Sew the borders to the quilt, mitering the corners (see "Mitered Borders" on pages 26–27).

Finishing

See "Finishing Techniques" on pages 30–32.

1. Mark the quilt top for quilting according to the quilting plan or as desired.
2. Layer the quilt top with the backing and batting; baste and quilt.
3. Trim the edges of the backing and batting even with the quilt top. Bind the edges.

Quilting Plan

Appliqué Templates and Placement Diagram

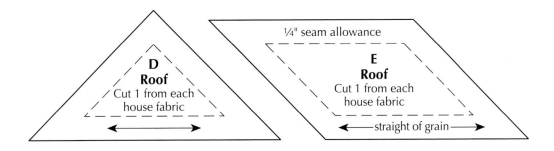

Bountiful Harvest

"Bountiful Harvest" was designed as a Thanksgiving quilt, but it quickly became a quilt I can seldom put away. The appliquéd center is reminiscent of the Album quilts of the mid-nineteenth century, and many of the fabrics recall that period as well. Appliqué, surrounded by sawtooth borders and plenty of open space for hand quilting, makes a delightful no-calorie feast!

While reproduction fabrics give "Bountiful Harvest" its nineteenth-century appeal, you may prefer a more contemporary look. Whatever you decide, choose fabrics that enhance the design. Use window templates to isolate sections of a large-scale print—you may find a spot that looks just like an apple or shaded colors perfect for the grapes, all in a single piece of fabric. Hand-dyed fabrics could also be effective and can be further embellished with permanent pens to add depth and detail.

Quilt Size: 21¼" × 21¼"

Materials: 42"-wide fabric:

⅝ yd. light for appliqué background, sawtooth borders A and C, and border B
⅝ yd. dark #1 for sawtooth borders A and C
½ yd. dark #2 for border D and binding
Assorted scraps for appliqués
¾ yd. fabric for backing
23" × 23" piece of batting

Cutting

All measurements include ¼"-wide seam allowances.

From the light fabric, cut:
1 oversize square, 10¼", for appliqué background
4 strips, each 2" × 14¾", for border B
1 rectangle, 18" × 22", for sawtooth borders A and C
1 strip, ⅞" × 12", for borders A and C center squares

From dark fabric #1, cut:
1 rectangle, 18" × 22", for sawtooth borders A and C
1 strip, ⅞" × 12", for borders A and C center squares
8 strips, each ⅞" × 14¾", for border B

From dark fabric #2, cut:
4 strips, each 3¼" × 22", for border D

Center Appliquéd Block

See "Appliquéing Small Quilts" on pages 11–19 for general appliqué techniques.

1. Fold the 10¼" square in quarters to find its center point, then crease the block on both diagonals. Referring to "Preparing Background Fabric" on page 13, prepare the square for appliqué. Use the appliqué placement diagram on page 70 as a guide.
2. From the appropriate appliqué fabric, cut a ½"-wide bias strip, approximately 8" long, for the stems (see "Stems and Vines" on page 19). Trim the strip as needed to cut the stems. Pin, then appliqué the stems to the block in alphabetical order. Be sure to keep all the appliqués within the 8¼" finished size of the block.

3. Using the templates on page 70, trace and cut a freezer-paper template for each appliqué shape. Because the appliqué block is asymmetrical, the paper templates must be reversed (see "Making Freezer-Paper Templates" on pages 14–15). Number the paper templates to correspond with the appliqué placement diagram.
4. Press each freezer-paper template to the wrong side of the appropriate appliqué fabric. Cut out the shapes, adding a 3⁄16" seam allowance all around, and baste the seam allowances as desired.
5. Pin or baste the pieces to the background block in numerical order, then appliqué. Remove the freezer-paper templates (see "Removing the Glue and Freezer Paper" on pages 18–19).
6. Trim and square up the completed block to measure 8¾" (see "Squaring Up the Blocks" on page 25).

Bias Squares

Borders A and C are made up of half-square triangle units called bias squares. The bias-square method is excellent for small-scale work. It is efficient and, most importantly, accurate because the squares are cut after the diagonal seam is sewn. Best of all, the squares are already pressed. Follow steps 1–5 to make 120 bias-square units, each 1¼", and 8 center-square units.

1. Place the light and dark 18" × 22" rectangles right sides together. Use a rotary cutter and ruler to cut the rectangles into 1⅜"-wide bias strips. Continue cutting strips until the combined length of all the pairs equals approximately 220". Do not separate the pairs.

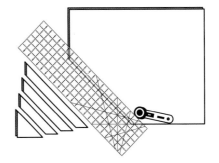

2. Sew each pair of strips together along one long bias edge, then trim the seam allowances to ⅛". Press the seam allowances toward the dark fabric. (I like to press the sewn pairs with spray starch.)

3. Place the bias-strip pairs seam side up. Use a Bias Square ruler and a fine-line permanent pen to mark as many 1¼" squares as will fit on each pair of bias strips. Position the Bias Square so that the diagonal line is on the seam line of the strip pair, and begin marking squares from the bottom. Marking the squares first, rather than simply cutting them, may seem tedious, but I find that for small bias-square units, it is more accurate. To keep track of the number of squares drawn on each bias-strip pair, mark the number in the margin at the top of the strip.

1¼" square

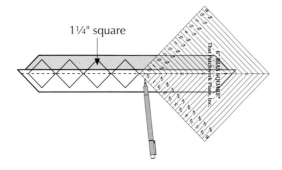

4. Cut the squares carefully, right on the line, using scissors or a rotary cutter.

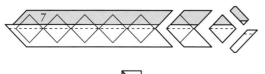

1¼" bias square

5. Place the light and dark ⅞" × 12" strips right sides together and sew along one long edge. Trim the seam allowance and press toward the dark fabric. Cut the pieced unit into 8 squares, each 1¼", for the center units of borders A and C.

1¼"

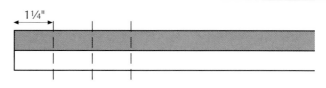

Borders A and C

1. Referring to the illustration below, make the border A side borders, using 10 bias squares and 1 center-square unit for each. Press the seam allowances away from the center square.

Side border A
Make 2.

2. Referring to the illustration below, make the border A top and bottom borders, using 12 bias squares and 1 center-square unit for each. Note that the bias squares at the ends are turned. Press the seam allowances away from the center squares.

Top and bottom border A
Make 2.

3. Repeat steps 1 and 2 to make border C, using 18 bias squares and 1 center-square unit for the sides and 20 bias squares and 1 center-square unit for the top and the bottom. Note that the bias squares at the ends of the top and bottom borders are *not* turned.

Side border C
Make 2.

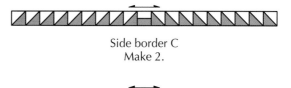

Top and bottom border C
Make 2.

Border B

Sew a ⅞" × 14¾" strip of dark #1 to each long side of the 2" × 14¾" light strips to make 4 border B units. Trim the seam allowances and press them toward the dark fabric.

Border B unit
Make 4.

Assembling the Quilt

1. Position the border A side borders along the left and right edges of the appliqué block. Pin at the center point, at each end, and at several places in between. Stitch, then press the seam allowances toward the center block. Pin, stitch, and press the top and bottom units of border A.

2. Sew a border B unit to each side of the quilt, mitering the corners (see "Mitered Borders" on pages 26–27).

Border B

3. Repeat step 1 for border C.
4. Sew a 3¼" × 22" border D strip to each side of the quilt. Miter the corners.

Finishing

See "Finishing Techniques" on pages 30–32.

1. Mark the quilt top for quilting according to the quilting plan or as desired.
2. Layer the quilt top with the backing and batting; baste and quilt.
3. Trim the edges of the backing and batting even with the quilt top. Bind the edges.

Quilting Plan

Appliqué Templates and Placement Diagram
Cut all templates in reverse.

Quilting Pattern
Border B

Center line

Center

Autumn Flight

Savor the last days of autumn by making a little quilt inspired by leaves falling from trees and geese winging south for the winter. The strippy set is a traditional one for scrappy Flying Geese. For variation, I reversed the direction of the geese in alternate rows, even though it does appear that some are headed the wrong way! The Flying Geese are pieced with a quick, accurate, cut-no-triangles method. I pieced the center of this quilt in just one day, then enjoyed taking my time with the appliqué border.

The more fabrics you use for the Flying Geese, the more old-fashioned your quilt will look. I used a lot of grayed colors in my quilt, so the gold geese add an important bit of sparkle. For an even more primitive look, try varying the background fabrics as well. It's best to use nondirectional fabrics for the Flying Geese background.

Select sashing fabric after the rows are pieced, auditioning the rows on different fabrics to find just the right one. Choose a fabric that frames the pieced rows without overwhelming them.

The outer border fabric is light, but still darker than the background, so the lighter, brighter pieced rows remain the focal point of the quilt.

Quilt Size: 21" × 24½"
Finished Flying Geese Unit Size: ¾" × 1½"

Materials: 42"-wide fabric

¼ yd. light for Flying Geese background

½ yd. *total* assorted scraps for Flying Geese and appliqués

½ yd. medium brown for sashing

⅛ yd. medium pink for inner border

¾ yd. light beige for outer border and binding

¼ yd. dark green for vine

¾ yd. fabric for backing

23" × 27" piece of batting

Cutting

All measurements include ¼"-wide seam allowances.

From the light fabric, cut:

200 squares, each 1¼", for Flying Geese backgrounds

From the assorted scraps, cut a total of:

100 rectangles, each 1¼" × 2", for "geese"

From the medium brown fabric, cut:

6 strips, each 1½" × 15½", on the *lengthwise* grain for vertical sashing

2 strips, each 1½" × 14", for horizontal sashing

From the medium pink fabric, cut:

2 strips, each 1" × 17½", for side inner borders

2 strips, each 1" × 15", for top and bottom inner borders

From the light beige fabric, cut:

2 overwide strips, each 4¾" × 18½", for side outer borders

2 overwide strips, each 4¾" × 24½", for top and bottom outer borders

Flying Geese Units and Rows

See "Piecing with Precision" on pages 20–24 for general construction techniques.

1. Draw a light line on the back of each 1¼" background square from corner to corner. This will be the sewing line, so accuracy counts!

2. Place a background square on a 1¼" × 2" rectangle, right sides together, with the top, bottom, and one side even.

Drawn line

3. Sew on the diagonal from one corner of the square to the other. Use the line as a guide, but stitch a needle's width outside it. The edge of the needle should just touch the line.

4. Trim the seam allowance to ⅛", and press the background piece away from the "goose" to form a new corner for the rectangle.

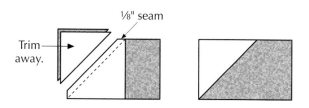

⅛" seam

Trim away.

5. Place another background square over the other corner of the rectangle (there will be a slight overlap). Sew, trim, and press to complete one unit.

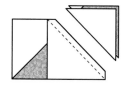
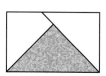

6. Repeat steps 2–5 to make 100 Flying Geese units.

7. Arrange the Flying Geese units in 5 vertical rows of 20 geese each. The second and fourth rows of geese fly opposite the rest.

    The stitching lines on the back of each unit cross to form an **X**. Sew the Flying Geese into rows, stitching through the center of the **X** for a perfect point. Press the seam allowances toward the geese fabrics.

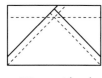

Wrong side of
Flying Geese unit

Assembling the Quilt

1. Lay out the quilt top, alternating 15½"-long sashing strips with pieced rows, beginning and ending with sashing strips as shown. Carefully pin the rows together, matching the center points and edges and aligning the geese horizontally from row to row. Stitch, then press the seam allowances toward the sashing.

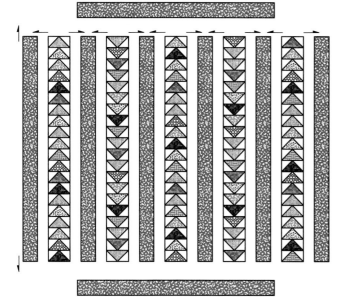

2. Pin and sew 14"-long sashing strips to the top and bottom of the quilt top. Press the seam allowance toward the sashing.

3. Add the medium pink inner borders, then the light beige outer borders to the quilt top (see "Straight-Cut Borders" on page 26).

Appliquéing the Border

See "Appliquéing Small Quilts" on pages 11–19 for general appliqué techniques.

1. Cut enough ½"-wide bias strips from the vine fabric to equal 110" in length. Join the strips by hand or machine. Press under a ³⁄₁₆" seam allowance all along one long edge.

2. Using the leaf template on page 74, make 116 freezer-paper templates. Press the templates to the wrong side of the appliqué fabrics. Cut out the leaves, adding a ³⁄₁₆" seam allowance around each, and baste the seams as desired.

3. Use the appliqué placement diagrams on pages 74–75 to trace the top and bottom, and then the side vine patterns onto the outer border. Mark a single line to represent the vine. Do not mark the leaves yet.

    Complete each vine segment by reversing (flipping) and matching the diagram at its midpoint to create a mirror image. Turn the corners by tracing the corner segment shown in the appliqué placement diagram on page 75, flipping the diagram as necessary to turn the corner smoothly.

    Pin or baste the vine in place, then appliqué the vine to the border (see "Stems and Vines" on page 19).

4. Use the appliqué placement diagrams on pages 74–75 as a guide to position the leaves along the vine. (Note: Although you have reversed the placement diagrams to position the vine, arrange the leaves so that they all face in the same direction. Refer to the quilt diagram on page 71 for additional guidance.) Use a dot to mark the placement of each leaf.

Appliqué the leaves to the border, then remove the freezer paper (see "Removing the Glue and Freezer Paper" on pages 18–19).

Finishing

See "Finishing Techniques" on pages 30–32.

1. Mark the quilt top for quilting according to the quilting plan or as desired.
2. Layer the quilt top with the backing and batting; baste and quilt.
3. Trim the edges of the backing, batting, and quilt top to 21" × 24¼". Bind the edges.

Quilting Plan

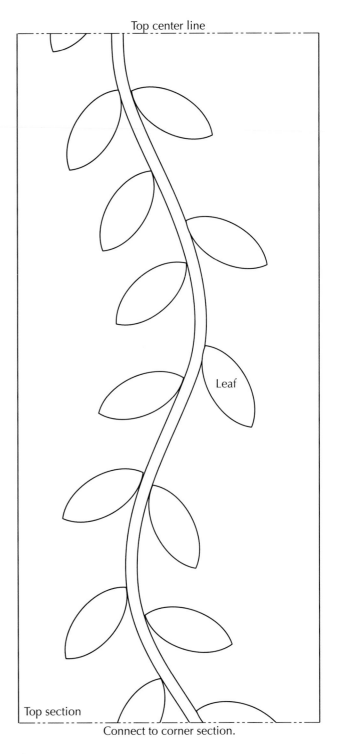

Top center line

Leaf

Top section

Connect to corner section.

Appliqué Templates and Placement Diagram

Connect to corner section.

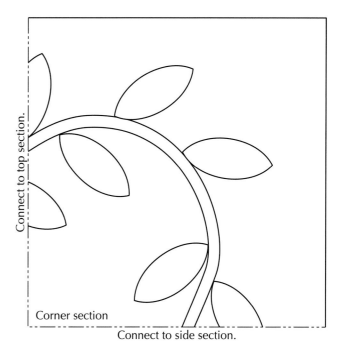

Connect to top section.

Corner section

Connect to side section.

Appliqué Templates and Placement Diagrams

Side section

Side center line

Sunbonnet Friends

Sunbonnet Sue and Overall Sam adorned my first quilt, the baby quilt I made for my son Russell (see page 4). I chose blue and yellow for the quilt and featured both Sue and Sam, since in those days we couldn't determine beforehand if the baby was a boy or girl. Russell loved his quilt, and despite some shortcomings in its design and workmanship, I'm pretty sentimental about it myself. Twenty years later, I decided to make "Sunbonnet Friends," a similar—but much smaller—version. I look forward to one day completing the circle by giving "Sunbonnet Friends" to Russell's child.

Quilt Size: 21" × 27"
Finished Block Size: 3"

❧ Making the little sunbonnet people is as much fun as playing paper dolls! Tiny plaids, checks, and stripes work well for Sam's overalls, and small floral prints are perfect for Sue's dresses. In my quilt, no two sunbonnets are the same, although I did repeat a few other fabrics here and there. Be sure that Sue's sleeve contrasts sharply with her dress and that Sam's shirt contrasts with his overalls.

Materials: 42"-wide fabric

⅝ yd. light for pieced blocks and appliqué backgrounds

⅜ yd. medium blue #1 for blocks and binding

⅜ yd. medium blue #2 for blocks and middle borders

⅝ yd. light blue for blocks and outer borders

¼ yd. yellow for inner border

¼ yd. *total* assorted blue and yellow scraps for appliqués

⅞ yd. fabric for backing

23" × 29" piece of batting

Cutting

All measurements include ¼"-wide seam allowances.

From the light fabric, cut:

17 oversize squares, each 4½", for appliqué backgrounds

144 squares, each 1¼", for triangle units (blocks)

From the medium blue #1 fabric, cut:

18 squares, each 2", for center squares (blocks)

From the medium blue #2 fabric, cut:

72 squares, each 1¼", for corner squares (blocks)

2 strips, each 1⅛" × 28", for side middle borders

2 strips, each 1⅛" × 22", for top and bottom middle borders

From the light blue fabric, cut:

72 rectangles, each 1¼" × 2", for triangle units (blocks)

2 strips, each 2½" × 28", for side outer borders

2 strips, each 2½" × 22", for top and bottom outer borders

From the yellow fabric, cut:

2 strips, each ⅞" × 28", for side inner borders

2 strips, each ⅞" × 22", for top and bottom inner borders

Pieced Blocks

See "Piecing with Precision" on pages 20–24 for general construction techniques. Press all seams as indicated by the arrows in the illustrations.

1. Use the 1¼" × 2" rectangles and the 1¼" background squares to make 72 triangle units. See "Flying Geese Units and Rows," steps 1–5, on page 72.

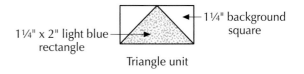

1¼" × 2" light blue rectangle — 1¼" background square

Triangle unit

2. Make 36 Row 1 units by sewing 2 medium blue #2 squares to a triangle unit as shown.

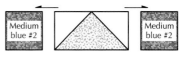

Medium blue #2 — Medium blue #2

Row 1

3. Make 18 Row 2 units by sewing 2 triangle units to a medium blue #1 square as shown.

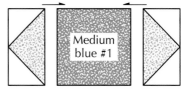

Medium blue #1

Row 2

4. Assemble the blocks by sewing Row 1 units to the top and bottom of each Row 2 unit. Be sure the rows are turned properly before you sew. Make 18 blocks.

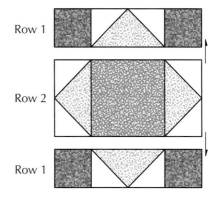

Row 1

Row 2

Row 1

Appliquéd Blocks

See "Appliquéing Small Quilts" on pages 11–19 for general appliqué techniques.

1. Fold each 4½" light square in quarters to find its center point, then crease the square on both diagonals. Referring to "Preparing Background Fabric" on page 13, prepare the blocks for appliqué. Use the appliqué placement diagrams on page 79 as a guide. You'll need 8 Sam blocks and 9 Sue blocks.

2. For each Sunbonnet Sue, make nine freezer-paper templates of appliqués 1–5. For Overall Sam, make eight freezer-paper templates of appliqués 6, 8, and 9, and sixteen of 7. Note that Sue is an asymmetrical pattern, so remember to reverse all the Sue templates (see "Making Freezer-Paper Templates" on pages 14–15).

3. Press each freezer-paper template to the wrong side of the appropriate appliqué fabric. Cut out the fabric shapes, adding a ³⁄₁₆" seam allowance all around. Baste the seam allowances as desired, then appliqué the pieces to the background blocks in numerical order. Be sure to keep the appliqués within the 3" finished size of the block.

   Make a total of 17 appliqué blocks: 8 of Sam and 9 of Sue. Remove the paper templates (see "Removing the Glue and Freezer Paper" on pages 18–19).

4. Trim and square up the completed appliqué blocks to measure 3½". (See "Squaring Up the Blocks" on page 25).

Note: *Be sure to measure your work. The dimensions of the appliqué blocks must match the dimensions of the pieced blocks.*

Assembling the Quilt

1. Arrange the blocks in 7 horizontal rows of 5 blocks each. Alternate pieced and appliquéd blocks, with a pieced block at each corner. Place Sam in the first row, Sue in the next, and so on.

2. Sew the blocks together, pressing the seam allowances toward the appliqué blocks. Pin, then sew the units into rows to form the quilt top. Press the seam allowances away from the center of the quilt.

Borders

1. Sew together a ⅞"-wide yellow inner border strip, a 1⅛"-wide medium blue #2 middle border strip, and a 2½"-wide light blue outer border strip, matching lengths, to make a border unit. Make 4 border units. Press the seam allowances toward the middle strip.

2. Sew the borders to the quilt top, mitering the corners (see "Mitered Borders" on pages 26–27).

Finishing

See "Finishing Techniques" on pages 30–32.

1. Mark the quilt top for quilting according to the quilting plan or as desired.
2. Layer the quilt top with the backing and batting; baste and quilt.
3. Trim the edges of the backing and batting even with the quilt top. Bind the edges.

Quilting Plan

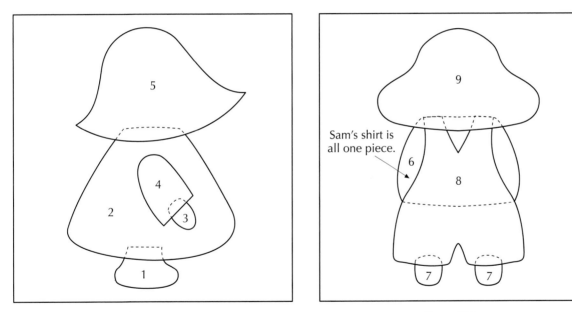

Sunbonnet Sue
Cut all templates in reverse.
Make 9.

Overall Sam
Make 8.

Sam's shirt is all one piece.

Appliqué Templates and Placement Diagrams

Teapot Traditions

When I'm not dreaming about quilts, I'm likely to be dreaming about England. How better to dream than over a hot cup of tea, poured from a pretty teapot? As a devoted Anglophile, I have loved and collected teapots—new and old—for many years. On trips to England, I always carry a quilted duffel bag, just right for bringing home a carefully protected pot or two.

Appliquéd teapots are not as fragile as the real thing, but they are almost as much fun to collect, so making a quilted cupboard filled with teapots was a pleasure. The teapot shapes are drawn from the pattern books of early English potters like Spode and Wedgwood, and are easier to appliqué than they might seem. Why not appliqué a collection for yourself? It won't take long, and when you are finished, be sure to treat yourself to a perfect pot of tea.

When I decided to make a teapot quilt, I began by collecting fabrics that reminded me of English dishes from the eighteenth and nineteenth centuries. (This may have been my favorite part of the process. I still can't resist buying "dish" fabric when I find it!) The teapot fabrics don't have to be blue and white. Just gather some small pieces that say "teapot" to you, then place the freezer-paper templates on the fabric so the appliqué will look as much as possible like a teapot.

Choose the background fabric carefully. It shouldn't be so busy that it draws attention from the teapots, and it must offer enough contrast that the teapots stand out.

Quilt Size: 17" × 17"

Materials: 42"-wide fabric

Fat quarter (18" × 22") light background

¼ yd. brown for shelves

⅜ yd. light blue for inner borders

⅝ yd. medium floral for outer borders and binding

4" × 6" pieces of 9 assorted fabrics for teapot appliqués

Assorted pink and green scraps for rose and leaf appliqués

½ yd. fabric for backing

19" × 19" piece of batting

Cutting

All measurements include ¼"-wide seam allowances.

From the light fabric, cut:
1 oversize square, 11¼", for teapot background

From the brown fabric, cut:
2 strips, each ⅞" × 10¼", for shelf sides
2 strips, each ⅞" × 11", for top and bottom shelves

From the light blue fabric, cut:
4 strips, each 4" × 18", for inner border

From the medium floral fabric, cut:
1 square, 18", for outer cutwork border

Center Appliquéd Block

See "Appliquéing Small Quilts" on pages 11–19 for general appliqué techniques. The glue and orange-stick methods work well for preparing the teapot appliqués. The shapes may seem tricky, but remember to turn under a tiny bit at a time and you'll do fine.

1. Fold the 11¼" square into quarters to find its center point, then crease the block on both diagonals. Use a square ruler and a water-soluble marking pen (or other removable marker) on the right side of the fabric to mark a 9¾" square in the middle of the block. These markings will be seam lines.

Measure 3" down from the top line and draw a horizontal line across the block. Measure 3⅜" down from that line and draw another horizontal line. These two marks are placement guidelines for the appliquéd shelves.

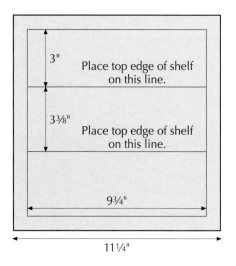

2. Because the appliqués are asymmetrical, the freezer-paper templates must be cut in reverse. Using the templates on page 85, make a reversed freezer-paper template for each teapot. Transfer the dotted center lines of Templates #2, #5, and #8 to the freezer-paper templates (see "Making Freezer-Paper Templates" on pages 14–15).

3. Press each freezer-paper template to the wrong side of the appropriate teapot fabric. Cut out the teapot shapes, adding a ³⁄₁₆" seam allowance all around. Don't try to cut into the handle holes or deep into the **V** where the spouts join the pots. Clip those areas later, after you apply the glue.

4. Use the gluestick method to turn back the edges of the teapots, clipping the seams carefully where needed (see "Glue Basting the Appliqués" on pages 16–17).

5. Make 2 freezer-paper templates of Template #10. Press the freezer-paper templates to the wrong side of the remaining brown fabric. Cut out the fabric shelves, adding a ³⁄₁₆" seam allowance along the top and bottom of the shelves, and a full ¼" seam allowance along the

short edges. Glue-baste the top and bottom seam allowances. Do not turn under the ends.

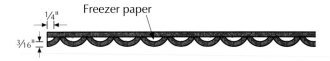
Freezer paper

6. Align the *top edges* of the shelf appliqués with the guidelines on the background block, and baste the appliqués in place. Do not skip the basting step! Appliqué the shelves to the background block.

7. Arrange the teapots on the shelves in numerical order. Use the photo on page 40 as a guide. Teapots 2, 5, and 8 are in the middle of their respective shelves. Center them by matching the dotted line on the template with the center crease on the block. Place a teapot on each side of the middle teapot, making sure that no teapot is closer than ¼" to the side seam line. The teapots in the top two rows should rest on the shelves, and the teapots in the bottom row should rest on the seam line. Pin or baste, then appliqué the teapots in place.

8. Soak the block to remove the glue, then remove the freezer-paper templates (see "Removing the Glue and Freezer Paper" on pages 18–19).

9. Trim and square up the background block to measure 10¼" (see "Squaring Up the Blocks" on page 25.)

Borders

See "Cutwork Appliqué Borders" on pages 27–29 for general instructions.

1. Sew a ⅞" × 10¼" brown strip to each side of the appliqué block. Press the seam allowance toward the brown fabric. Sew ⅞" × 11" brown strips to the top and the bottom of the appliqué block, pressing the seam allowances toward the brown fabric.

2. Fold each light blue strip in half to find its center point. Use Templates #11–#18 on page 84 to make *reverse* templates and cut fabric shapes for the rose. Baste the seams as desired. Position the rose in the middle of an inner border strip, so that the leaves are ¼" above the seam line. Use the appliqué placement diagram on page 84 as a guide (see "Preparing Background Fabric" on page 13).

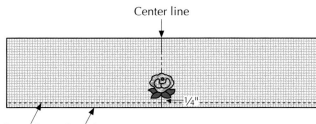
Center line
Seam line   Cut edge

3. Appliqué the rose to the strip in numerical order.

4. Sew the inner borders to the quilt, mitering the corners. Place the border with the rose

appliqué at the top edge (see "Mitered Borders" on pages 26–27).

5. Cut a 17" square of freezer paper. Fold the paper in quarters, creasing the folds. Fold once more, on the diagonal, dividing the square into 8 equal triangles. Hold the triangle of paper so the diagonal fold is on your left. Put an identification mark on the section of the paper that is facing you.

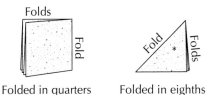

Folded in quarters   Folded in eighths

6. Unfold the square. Using the template on page 84, make a freezer-paper template for the outer border. Place the template on the corner of the paper with the identification mark as shown. Trace the outer border template onto the paper.

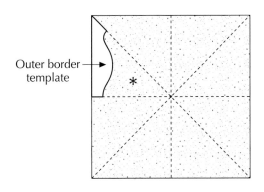

7. Refold the freezer-paper square so that the traced line is on the outside. Carefully cut on the curved line. *Do not cut the folds!*

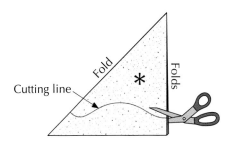

Unfold the paper. You will have a full-size template for the outer border.

8. Center the paper template on the right side of the 18" square of medium floral fabric. There should be a ½" seam allowance all around the outside of the paper square. Press the template onto the fabric. Draw a fine line all around the curved edge of the template.

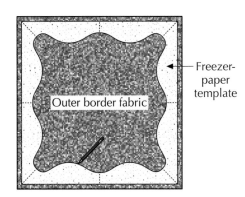

9. Remove the paper template. Cut out the middle of the fabric square, leaving a ³⁄₁₆" seam allowance beyond the drawn line. Turn under the seam allowance all around the curved line, basting it in place and clipping as necessary. Press.

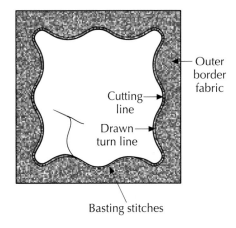

Basting stitches

10. Lay the outer border over the quilt top, aligning all outer edges and matching the centers and diagonal corner lines. Baste the outer border in place, then appliqué the curved edge

of the outer border to the inner border. Trim the inner border fabric behind the outer border.

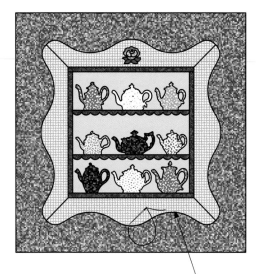

Appliqué.

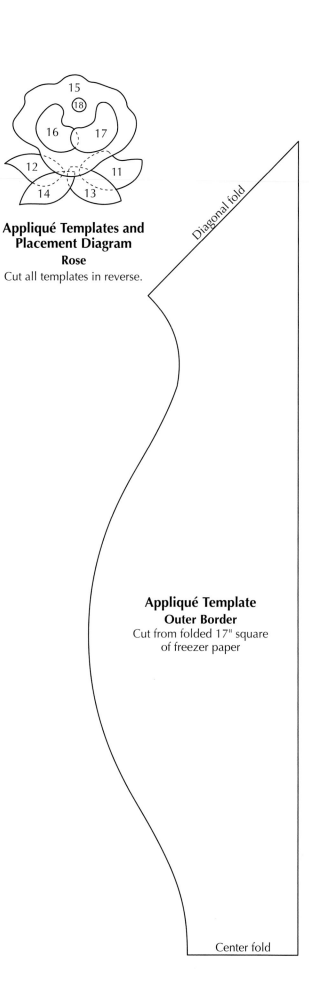

Appliqué Templates and Placement Diagram
Rose
Cut all templates in reverse.

Appliqué Template
Outer Border
Cut from folded 17" square of freezer paper

Finishing

See "Finishing Techniques" on pages 30–32.

1. Mark the quilt top for quilting according to the quilting plan or as desired.
2. Layer the quilt top with the backing and batting; baste and quilt.
3. Trim the quilt top, backing, and batting to measure 17" × 17". Bind the edges.

Quilting Plan

10
Shelf

1

2

5

3

4

6

8

7

9

Appliqué Templates

Cut all teapots in reverse.

Irish Rose

The Irish Chain has always been my favorite pieced pattern. I love its simplicity and strong diagonal line. My first rotary-cut and strip-pieced quilt was an Irish Chain, a perfect pattern for learning those techniques. In the years since, I've made dozens of them—big and small—and it is still the first pattern that comes to mind when I need a baby quilt in a hurry.

The crossing chains frame lots of open space perfect for appliqué. In "Irish Rose," two old favorites—the pieced Irish Chain and a traditional Rose of Sharon—combine to make a delightful small quilt, quick to piece and a pleasure to appliqué.

❧ *For my "not for Christmas only" Irish Rose, I chose the traditional reds and greens of the Rose of Sharon. Pastels would give the quilt an even more romantic feel.*

Because "Irish Rose" is strip pieced, it is best to avoid linear fabrics like checks and stripes. The values of the chain fabrics (A, B, and C) should contrast strongly. For the background, choose a light fabric that won't compete visually with the appliqué pattern. I used a tan solid, but a soft tone-on-tone or a bright white would also work well.

Quilt Size: 25¾" × 25¾"
Finished Block Size: 3¾"

Materials: 42"-wide fabric

½ yd. light (C) for blocks and appliqué backgrounds
½ yd. medium green (B) for blocks
Fat quarter (18" × 22") dark red (A) for blocks
¼ yd. gold for inner border
¼ yd. green for middle border
⅝ yd. red print for outer border and binding
¼ yd. dark green for large leaf appliqués
⅛ yd. gold for small leaf and rose center appliqués
⅛ yd. dark red for rose appliqués
⅞ yd. fabric for backing
28" × 28" piece of batting

Cutting

All measurements include ¼"-wide seam allowances.

From the light fabric (C), cut:
4 strips, each 1¼" × 18", for Block 1
3 strips, each 2¾" × 18", for Block 2
2 strips, each 5¼" × 18", for Block 2

From the medium green fabric (B), cut:
12 strips, each 1¼" × 18", for Block 1
6 strips, each 1¾" × 18", for Block 2

From the dark red fabric (A), cut:
9 strips, each 1¼" × 18", for Block 1

From the gold border fabric, cut:
4 strips, each ¾" × 27", for inner borders

From the green for the middle border, cut:
4 strips, each 1½" × 27", for middle borders

From the red print, cut:
4 strips, each 2¾" × 27", for outer borders

Fabric A   Fabric B   Fabric C

Piecing

Two blocks make the Irish Chain pattern. Block 1 is entirely pieced. Block 2 is pieced, then appliquéd. To avoid fraying or stretching that might occur as you appliqué, Block 2 is made over-sized, then trimmed to the correct size after the appliqué is complete.

See "Piecing with Precision" on pages 20–24 for general construction techniques.

Block 1

1. Using 1¼"-wide strips, place an A and a B strip right sides together, and stitch along one long edge. Make 9 pairs of A and B strips. Press the seam allowances toward the B strip.
2. Arrange the pairs of strips with the remaining 1¼"-wide strips to make strip sets as shown for Rows 1, 2, and 3. Sew the strips together, making 2 sets each for Rows 1 and 2, and 1 set for Row 3. Press each seam allowance toward the B strip before adding another strip to the set.

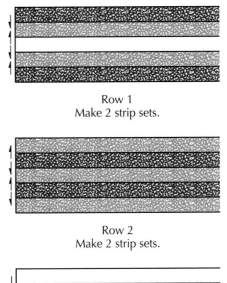

Row 1
Make 2 strip sets.

Row 2
Make 2 strip sets.

Row 3
Make 1 strip set.

3. Crosscut each strip set into 1¼"-wide rows. You need 26 each of Rows 1 and 2 and 13 of Row 3. You will have some leftovers.

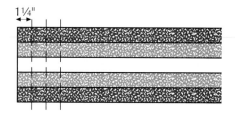

1¼"

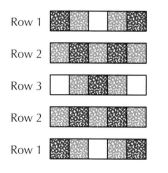

🌿 *To cut the strip sets into rows quickly, layer a Row 1 and a Row 2 strip set, right sides together, on the cutting mat. They should nest together perfectly. Cut across them, cutting them into rows. Do not separate the nested pairs after cutting. They are ready to be sewn together in the next step.*

4. Lay out and assemble Block 1 as shown, pressing the seams in the direction of the arrows. Make 13 of Block 1.

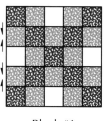

Row 1
Row 2
Row 3
Row 2
Row 1

Block #1

Block 2

1. To make a strip set for Row 1, sew a 1¾" × 18" B strip to each long edge of a 2¾" × 18" C strip. Make 3 strip sets. Press the seam allowances toward the B strips.

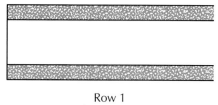

Row 1
Make 3 strip sets.

2. Crosscut each strip set into 1¾"-wide rows. You need 24 rows.

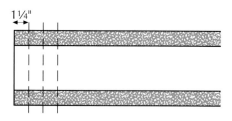

1¼"

3. Crosscut each 5¼" × 18" C strip into 2¾"-wide rows. You need 12 rows.

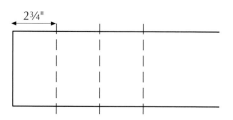

2¾"

4. Lay out and assemble Block 2 as shown, pressing the seams in the direction of the arrows. Make 12 of Block 2.

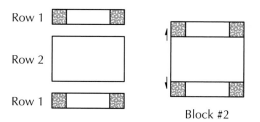

Row 1
Row 2
Row 1

Block #2

Appliqué

See "Appliquéing Small Quilts" on pages 11–19 for general appliqué techniques.

1. Prepare each Block 2 for appliqué. Use the appliqué placement diagram on page 90 as a guide (see "Preparing Background Fabric" on page 13).

2. Make 48 freezer-paper templates for Templates #1 and #4. Make 12 templates for Templates #2 and #3. Because these blocks are small and symmetrical, it is especially important that the paper templates be accurate. Make a plastic template of half of each shape first, and cut the freezer-paper on the fold (see "Making Freezer-Paper Templates" on pages 14–15).

3. Press the freezer-paper template to the wrong side of each appropriate appliqué fabric. Cut out the fabric appliqués, adding a 3⁄16" seam allowance all around, and baste the seams as desired.

4. Pin, then appliqué the pieces to the background blocks in numerical order. Remove the paper templates (see "Removing the Glue and Freezer Paper" on pages 18–19).

5. Trim and square up all the completed blocks to measure 4¼" (see "Squaring Up the Blocks" on page 25).

Assembling the Quilt

1. Arrange the blocks in 5 horizontal rows of 5 blocks each as shown. Begin with Block 1 at each corner, and alternate pieced and appliquéd blocks.

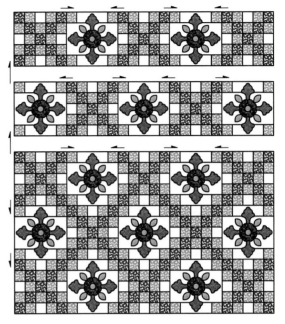

Assembly Diagram

2. Sew the blocks together, pressing the seam allowances toward Block 2. Pin carefully, then join the rows to form the quilt top. Press seam allowance away from the center of quilt.

Borders

1. To make a border unit, sew together a ¾"-wide gold strip, a 1½"-wide green strip, and a 2¾"-wide red strip. Make 4 border units, and press the seam allowances toward the middle strip.

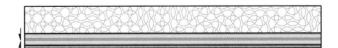

2. Sew the borders to each side of the quilt, mitering the corners (see "Mitered Borders" on pages 26–27).

Finishing

See "Finishing Techniques" on pages 30–32.

1. Mark the quilt top for quilting according to the quilting plan or as desired.
2. Layer the quilt top with the backing and batting; baste and quilt.
3. When the quilting is complete, trim the edges of the backing and batting even with the quilt top. Bind the edges.

Quilting Plan

Appliqué Templates and Placement Diagram

Bridal Wreath

About eighteen years ago, I decided to make a full-size quilt of 12" Bridal Wreath blocks. I began enthusiastically, but not surprisingly, my enthusiasm began to flag. Forty-eight large blocks, all the same, got to be more of a chore than a pleasure, and soon my closet held another false start.

Time passed, and I still wanted a Bridal Wreath quilt, so many years later I began again. Remembering my false start, this Bridal Wreath would be much smaller, and for variety, it would include a simple connecting block with fewer pieces to sew. Making this small quilt was a pleasure, never a chore, and best of all, I finished it!

Bridal Wreath is a cheerful pattern that was popular in the 1930s, so using reproduction fabrics and a muslin background was a natural choice. I loved working with these fabrics. Their fresh charm was cheering on the often gray winter days I spent appliquéing the blocks.

You can make the blocks as scrappy as you wish, or you can use a limited fabric selection as I did. I used three different blues and three different pinks for the hearts, and four different leaf fabrics. All my Wreath and Vine blocks are identical. If you use pastels, be sure they will show up against the background fabric, and take care that the vine fabric does not overpower the appliqués.

Quilt Size: 35" × 35"
Finished Block Size: 5"

Materials: 42"-wide fabric

1¾ yds. light for appliqué background and inner borders

⅞ yd. pastel print for outer borders and binding

¼ yd. medium green #1 for narrow inner borders

⅜ yd. medium green #2 for vines and wreaths

¼ yd. *total* assorted pastels for leaf appliqués

⅓ yd. *total* assorted pastels for heart appliqués

1⅛ yds. fabric for backing

37" × 37" piece of batting

Cutting

All measurements include ¼"-wide seam allowances.

From the light fabric, cut:

25 oversize squares, each 6½", for appliqué backgrounds

4 strips, each 5" × 37", for wide inner borders

From the pastel border fabric, cut:

4 strips, each 4¾" × 37", for outer borders

From medium green #1, cut:

4 strips, each ⅞" × 37", for the narrow inner borders

From medium green #2, cut:

13 bias strips, each ½" × 10", for wreaths

48 bias strips, each ½" × 3", for vines

Appliqué

See "Appliquéing Small Quilts" on pages 11–19 for general appliqué techniques.

1. Fold each 6½" background square into quarters to find its center point, then crease the block on both diagonals. Referring to "Preparing Background Fabric" on page 13, prepare the background blocks for appliqué. Use the appliqué placement diagrams on pages 93 and 95 as guides. You need 12 Vine blocks and 13 Wreath blocks.

2. Make 156 freezer-paper templates for the leaves and 200 templates for the hearts. The leaf template is asymmetrical; cut it in reverse.

3. Press each freezer-paper template to the wrong side of the appropriate appliqué fabric. Cut out the fabric appliqués, adding a ³⁄₁₆" seam allowance all around, and baste the seams as desired.

4. Appliqué the bias strips to the background blocks, forming the wreaths and the vine sections (see "Stems and Vines" on page 19).

5. Pin or baste the leaves and hearts to the background blocks, then appliqué. Remove the freezer-paper templates (see "Removing the Glue and Freezer Paper" on pages 18–19).

6. Trim and square up the blocks to measure 5½" (see "Squaring Up the Blocks" on page 25.)

Assembling the Quilt

1. Arrange the blocks in 5 rows of 5 blocks each as shown. Begin with a Wreath block in each corner, and alternate the Wreath and Vine blocks.

2. Sew the blocks together, pressing the seams open. Pin carefully, then join the rows to form the quilt top. Press the seam allowances open.

Assembly Diagram

Borders

See "Cutwork Appliqué Borders" on pages 27–29 for general instructions.

1. Sew a ⅞"-wide green inner border strip to each of the 5"-wide light inner border strips. Trim the seam allowances and press them toward the narrow strips.

2. Sew the borders to the quilt, mitering the corners (see "Mitered Borders" on pages 26–27).

3. Using the outer border template on page 94 and the 4¾"-wide pastel border strips, baste, trim, and appliqué the cutwork borders.

Finishing

See "Finishing Techniques" on pages 30–32.

1. Mark the quilt top for quilting according to the quilting plan (space the grid lines ½" apart).

2. Layer the quilt top with the backing and batting; baste and quilt.

3. Trim the quilt top, backing, and batting to measure 35" × 35". Bind the edges.

Quilting Plan

**Appliqué
Placement Diagram
Vine Block**

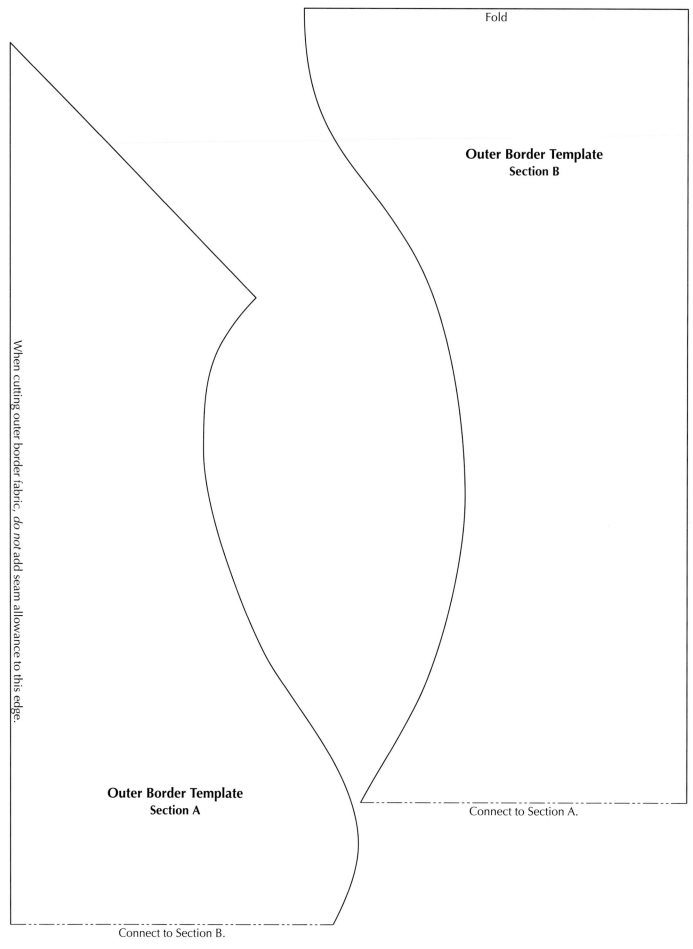

Fold

Outer Border Template
Section B

When cutting outer border fabric, *do not add seam allowance to this edge.*

Outer Border Template
Section A

Connect to Section A.

Connect to Section B.

Appliqué Templates and Placement Diagram
Wreath Block
Cut leaf templates in reverse.

ABOUT THE AUTHOR

Since making her first quilt in 1978, Elizabeth Hamby Carlson has made more quilts than she can count, and always has at least a dozen more in the planning stages. She began teaching quiltmaking in 1983 and especially enjoys sharing her methods of hand appliqué, miniature quilt-making, and hand quilting with new quilters. Through her pattern business, Elizabeth Quilts, she markets original quilt patterns that reflect her interest in the decorative arts and eighteenth- and nineteenth-century quiltmaking. In addition to her small traditional quilts, Elizabeth, a life-long Anglophile, also likes to design and make quilts inspired by her interest in English history. Her award-winning quilts have been featured in *Miniature Quilts* magazine and the *Quilt Art Engagement Calendar* and have been exhibited in England and across the United States.

Raised in northeastern Ohio, Elizabeth lives with her husband in Montgomery Village, Maryland. She has a grown daughter and son, each of whom has lots of quilts. When Elizabeth is not quilting, she enjoys reading, antiquing, and planning her next trip to England.